C-2980   CAREER EXAMINATION SERIES

This is your
PASSBOOK for...

Legal Assistant

Test Preparation Study Guide
Questions & Answers

COPYRIGHT NOTICE

This book is SOLELY intended for, is sold ONLY to, and its use is RESTRICTED to individual, bona fide applicants or candidates who qualify by virtue of having seriously filed applications for appropriate license, certificate, professional and/or promotional advancement, higher school matriculation, scholarship, or other legitimate requirements of education and/or governmental authorities.

This book is NOT intended for use, class instruction, tutoring, training, duplication, copying, reprinting, excerption, or adaptation, etc., by:

1) Other publishers
2) Proprietors and/or Instructors of "Coaching" and/or Preparatory Courses
3) Personnel and/or Training Divisions of commercial, industrial, and governmental organizations
4) Schools, colleges, or universities and/or their departments and staffs, including teachers and other personnel
5) Testing Agencies or Bureaus
6) Study groups which seek by the purchase of a single volume to copy and/or duplicate and/or adapt this material for use by the group as a whole without having purchased individual volumes for each of the members of the group
7) Et al.

Such persons would be in violation of appropriate Federal and State statutes.

PROVISION OF LICENSING AGREEMENTS – Recognized educational, commercial, industrial, and governmental institutions and organizations, and others legitimately engaged in educational pursuits, including training, testing, and measurement activities, may address request for a licensing agreement to the copyright owners, who will determine whether, and under what conditions, including fees and charges, the materials in this book may be used them. In other words, a licensing facility exists for the legitimate use of the material in this book on other than an individual basis. However, it is asseverated and affirmed here that the material in this book CANNOT be used without the receipt of the express permission of such a licensing agreement from the Publishers. Inquiries re licensing should be addressed to the company, attention rights and permissions department.

All rights reserved, including the right of reproduction in whole or in part, in any form or by any means, electronic or mechanical, including photocopying, recording, or by any information storage and retrieval system, without permission in writing from the Publisher.

Copyright © 2024 by
National Learning Corporation

212 Michael Drive, Syosset, NY 11791
(516) 921-8888 • www.passbooks.com
E-mail: info@passbooks.com

PUBLISHED IN THE UNITED STATES OF AMERICA

PASSBOOK® SERIES

THE *PASSBOOK® SERIES* has been created to prepare applicants and candidates for the ultimate academic battlefield – the examination room.

At some time in our lives, each and every one of us may be required to take an examination – for validation, matriculation, admission, qualification, registration, certification, or licensure.

Based on the assumption that every applicant or candidate has met the basic formal educational standards, has taken the required number of courses, and read the necessary texts, the *PASSBOOK® SERIES* furnishes the one special preparation which may assure passing with confidence, instead of failing with insecurity. Examination questions – together with answers – are furnished as the basic vehicle for study so that the mysteries of the examination and its compounding difficulties may be eliminated or diminished by a sure method.

This book is meant to help you pass your examination provided that you qualify and are serious in your objective.

The entire field is reviewed through the huge store of content information which is succinctly presented through a provocative and challenging approach – the question-and-answer method.

A climate of success is established by furnishing the correct answers at the end of each test.

You soon learn to recognize types of questions, forms of questions, and patterns of questioning. You may even begin to anticipate expected outcomes.

You perceive that many questions are repeated or adapted so that you can gain acute insights, which may enable you to score many sure points.

You learn how to confront new questions, or types of questions, and to attack them confidently and work out the correct answers.

You note objectives and emphases, and recognize pitfalls and dangers, so that you may make positive educational adjustments.

Moreover, you are kept fully informed in relation to new concepts, methods, practices, and directions in the field.

You discover that you are actually taking the examination all the time: you are preparing for the examination by "taking" an examination, not by reading extraneous and/or supererogatory textbooks.

In short, this PASSBOOK®, used directedly, should be an important factor in helping you to pass your test.

LEGAL ASSISTANT

DUTIES
Assists in performing paralegal work, preparing simple legal documents, and performing legal research not requiring professional legal competence; performs related duties as required.

SCOPE OF THE EXAMINATION
The written test will cover knowledge, skills and/or abilities in such areas as:

1. Evaluating conditions in light of known facts;
2. Grammar/usage/punctuation;
3. Legal terminology, documents and forms;
4. Office record keeping;
5. Preparing written material; and
6. Understanding and interpreting legal material.

HOW TO TAKE A TEST

I. YOU MUST PASS AN EXAMINATION

A. WHAT EVERY CANDIDATE SHOULD KNOW

Examination applicants often ask us for help in preparing for the written test. What can I study in advance? What kinds of questions will be asked? How will the test be given? How will the papers be graded?

As an applicant for a civil service examination, you may be wondering about some of these things. Our purpose here is to suggest effective methods of advance study and to describe civil service examinations.

Your chances for success on this examination can be increased if you know how to prepare. Those "pre-examination jitters" can be reduced if you know what to expect. You can even experience an adventure in good citizenship if you know why civil service exams are given.

B. WHY ARE CIVIL SERVICE EXAMINATIONS GIVEN?

Civil service examinations are important to you in two ways. As a citizen, you want public jobs filled by employees who know how to do their work. As a job seeker, you want a fair chance to compete for that job on an equal footing with other candidates. The best-known means of accomplishing this two-fold goal is the competitive examination.

Exams are widely publicized throughout the nation. They may be administered for jobs in federal, state, city, municipal, town or village governments or agencies.

Any citizen may apply, with some limitations, such as the age or residence of applicants. Your experience and education may be reviewed to see whether you meet the requirements for the particular examination. When these requirements exist, they are reasonable and applied consistently to all applicants. Thus, a competitive examination may cause you some uneasiness now, but it is your privilege and safeguard.

C. HOW ARE CIVIL SERVICE EXAMS DEVELOPED?

Examinations are carefully written by trained technicians who are specialists in the field known as "psychological measurement," in consultation with recognized authorities in the field of work that the test will cover. These experts recommend the subject matter areas or skills to be tested; only those knowledges or skills important to your success on the job are included. The most reliable books and source materials available are used as references. Together, the experts and technicians judge the difficulty level of the questions.

Test technicians know how to phrase questions so that the problem is clearly stated. Their ethics do not permit "trick" or "catch" questions. Questions may have been tried out on sample groups, or subjected to statistical analysis, to determine their usefulness.

Written tests are often used in combination with performance tests, ratings of training and experience, and oral interviews. All of these measures combine to form the best-known means of finding the right person for the right job.

II. HOW TO PASS THE WRITTEN TEST

A. NATURE OF THE EXAMINATION

To prepare intelligently for civil service examinations, you should know how they differ from school examinations you have taken. In school you were assigned certain definite pages to read or subjects to cover. The examination questions were quite detailed and usually emphasized memory. Civil service exams, on the other hand, try to discover your present ability to perform the duties of a position, plus your potentiality to learn these duties. In other words, a civil service exam attempts to predict how successful you will be. Questions cover such a broad area that they cannot be as minute and detailed as school exam questions.

In the public service similar kinds of work, or positions, are grouped together in one "class." This process is known as *position-classification*. All the positions in a class are paid according to the salary range for that class. One class title covers all of these positions, and they are all tested by the same examination.

B. FOUR BASIC STEPS

1) Study the announcement

How, then, can you know what subjects to study? Our best answer is: "Learn as much as possible about the class of positions for which you've applied." The exam will test the knowledge, skills and abilities needed to do the work.

Your most valuable source of information about the position you want is the official exam announcement. This announcement lists the training and experience qualifications. Check these standards and apply only if you come reasonably close to meeting them.

The brief description of the position in the examination announcement offers some clues to the subjects which will be tested. Think about the job itself. Review the duties in your mind. Can you perform them, or are there some in which you are rusty? Fill in the blank spots in your preparation.

Many jurisdictions preview the written test in the exam announcement by including a section called "Knowledge and Abilities Required," "Scope of the Examination," or some similar heading. Here you will find out specifically what fields will be tested.

2) Review your own background

Once you learn in general what the position is all about, and what you need to know to do the work, ask yourself which subjects you already know fairly well and which need improvement. You may wonder whether to concentrate on improving your strong areas or on building some background in your fields of weakness. When the announcement has specified "some knowledge" or "considerable knowledge," or has used adjectives like "beginning principles of…" or "advanced … methods," you can get a clue as to the number and difficulty of questions to be asked in any given field. More questions, and hence broader coverage, would be included for those subjects which are more important in the work. Now weigh your strengths and weaknesses against the job requirements and prepare accordingly.

3) Determine the level of the position

Another way to tell how intensively you should prepare is to understand the level of the job for which you are applying. Is it the entering level? In other words, is this the position in which beginners in a field of work are hired? Or is it an intermediate or advanced level? Sometimes this is indicated by such words as "Junior" or "Senior" in the class title. Other jurisdictions use Roman numerals to designate the level – Clerk I, Clerk II, for example. The word "Supervisor" sometimes appears in the title. If the level is not indicated by the title, check the description of duties. Will you be working under very close supervision, or will you have responsibility for independent decisions in this work?

4) Choose appropriate study materials

Now that you know the subjects to be examined and the relative amount of each subject to be covered, you can choose suitable study materials. For beginning level jobs, or even advanced ones, if you have a pronounced weakness in some aspect of your training, read a modern, standard textbook in that field. Be sure it is up to date and has general coverage. Such books are normally available at your library, and the librarian will be glad to help you locate one. For entry-level positions, questions of appropriate difficulty are chosen – neither highly advanced questions, nor those too simple. Such questions require careful thought but not advanced training.

If the position for which you are applying is technical or advanced, you will read more advanced, specialized material. If you are already familiar with the basic principles of your field, elementary textbooks would waste your time. Concentrate on advanced textbooks and technical periodicals. Think through the concepts and review difficult problems in your field.

These are all general sources. You can get more ideas on your own initiative, following these leads. For example, training manuals and publications of the government agency which employs workers in your field can be useful, particularly for technical and professional positions. A letter or visit to the government department involved may result in more specific study suggestions, and certainly will provide you with a more definite idea of the exact nature of the position you are seeking.

III. KINDS OF TESTS

Tests are used for purposes other than measuring knowledge and ability to perform specified duties. For some positions, it is equally important to test ability to make adjustments to new situations or to profit from training. In others, basic mental abilities not dependent on information are essential. Questions which test these things may not appear as pertinent to the duties of the position as those which test for knowledge and information. Yet they are often highly important parts of a fair examination. For very general questions, it is almost impossible to help you direct your study efforts. What we can do is to point out some of the more common of these general abilities needed in public service positions and describe some typical questions.

1) General information

Broad, general information has been found useful for predicting job success in some kinds of work. This is tested in a variety of ways, from vocabulary lists to questions about current events. Basic background in some field of work, such as sociology or economics, may be sampled in a group of questions. Often these are principles which have become familiar to most persons through exposure rather than through formal training. It is difficult to advise you how to study for these questions; being alert to the world around you is our best suggestion.

2) Verbal ability

An example of an ability needed in many positions is verbal or language ability. Verbal ability is, in brief, the ability to use and understand words. Vocabulary and grammar tests are typical measures of this ability. Reading comprehension or paragraph interpretation questions are common in many kinds of civil service tests. You are given a paragraph of written material and asked to find its central meaning.

3) Numerical ability

Number skills can be tested by the familiar arithmetic problem, by checking paired lists of numbers to see which are alike and which are different, or by interpreting charts and graphs. In the latter test, a graph may be printed in the test booklet which you are asked to use as the basis for answering questions.

4) Observation

A popular test for law-enforcement positions is the observation test. A picture is shown to you for several minutes, then taken away. Questions about the picture test your ability to observe both details and larger elements.

5) Following directions

In many positions in the public service, the employee must be able to carry out written instructions dependably and accurately. You may be given a chart with several columns, each column listing a variety of information. The questions require you to carry out directions involving the information given in the chart.

6) Skills and aptitudes

Performance tests effectively measure some manual skills and aptitudes. When the skill is one in which you are trained, such as typing or shorthand, you can practice. These tests are often very much like those given in business school or high school courses. For many of the other skills and aptitudes, however, no short-time preparation can be made. Skills and abilities natural to you or that you have developed throughout your lifetime are being tested.

Many of the general questions just described provide all the data needed to answer the questions and ask you to use your reasoning ability to find the answers. Your best preparation for these tests, as well as for tests of facts and ideas, is to be at your physical and mental best. You, no doubt, have your own methods of getting into an exam-taking mood and keeping "in shape." The next section lists some ideas on this subject.

IV. KINDS OF QUESTIONS

Only rarely is the "essay" question, which you answer in narrative form, used in civil service tests. Civil service tests are usually of the short-answer type. Full instructions for answering these questions will be given to you at the examination. But in case this is your first experience with short-answer questions and separate answer sheets, here is what you need to know:

1) Multiple-choice Questions

Most popular of the short-answer questions is the "multiple choice" or "best answer" question. It can be used, for example, to test for factual knowledge, ability to solve problems or judgment in meeting situations found at work.

A multiple-choice question is normally one of three types—

- It can begin with an incomplete statement followed by several possible endings. You are to find the one ending which *best* completes the statement, although some of the others may not be entirely wrong.
- It can also be a complete statement in the form of a question which is answered by choosing one of the statements listed.

- It can be in the form of a problem – again you select the best answer.

Here is an example of a multiple-choice question with a discussion which should give you some clues as to the method for choosing the right answer:

When an employee has a complaint about his assignment, the action which will *best* help him overcome his difficulty is to
- A. discuss his difficulty with his coworkers
- B. take the problem to the head of the organization
- C. take the problem to the person who gave him the assignment
- D. say nothing to anyone about his complaint

In answering this question, you should study each of the choices to find which is best. Consider choice "A" – Certainly an employee may discuss his complaint with fellow employees, but no change or improvement can result, and the complaint remains unresolved. Choice "B" is a poor choice since the head of the organization probably does not know what assignment you have been given, and taking your problem to him is known as "going over the head" of the supervisor. The supervisor, or person who made the assignment, is the person who can clarify it or correct any injustice. Choice "C" is, therefore, correct. To say nothing, as in choice "D," is unwise. Supervisors have and interest in knowing the problems employees are facing, and the employee is seeking a solution to his problem.

2) True/False Questions

The "true/false" or "right/wrong" form of question is sometimes used. Here a complete statement is given. Your job is to decide whether the statement is right or wrong.

SAMPLE: A roaming cell-phone call to a nearby city costs less than a non-roaming call to a distant city.

This statement is wrong, or false, since roaming calls are more expensive.

This is not a complete list of all possible question forms, although most of the others are variations of these common types. You will always get complete directions for answering questions. Be sure you understand *how* to mark your answers – ask questions until you do.

V. RECORDING YOUR ANSWERS

Computer terminals are used more and more today for many different kinds of exams.

For an examination with very few applicants, you may be told to record your answers in the test booklet itself. Separate answer sheets are much more common. If this separate answer sheet is to be scored by machine – and this is often the case – it is highly important that you mark your answers correctly in order to get credit.

An electronic scoring machine is often used in civil service offices because of the speed with which papers can be scored. Machine-scored answer sheets must be marked with a pencil, which will be given to you. This pencil has a high graphite content which responds to the electronic scoring machine. As a matter of fact, stray dots may register as answers, so do not let your pencil rest on the answer sheet while you are pondering the correct answer. Also, if your pencil lead breaks or is otherwise defective, ask for another.

Since the answer sheet will be dropped in a slot in the scoring machine, be careful not to bend the corners or get the paper crumpled.

The answer sheet normally has five vertical columns of numbers, with 30 numbers to a column. These numbers correspond to the question numbers in your test booklet. After each number, going across the page are four or five pairs of dotted lines. These short dotted lines have small letters or numbers above them. The first two pairs may also have a "T" or "F" above the letters. This indicates that the first two pairs only are to be used if the questions are of the true-false type. If the questions are multiple choice, disregard the "T" and "F" and pay attention only to the small letters or numbers.

Answer your questions in the manner of the sample that follows:

32. The largest city in the United States is
    A. Washington, D.C.
    B. New York City
    C. Chicago
    D. Detroit
    E. San Francisco

1) Choose the answer you think is best. (New York City is the largest, so "B" is correct.)
2) Find the row of dotted lines numbered the same as the question you are answering. (Find row number 32)
3) Find the pair of dotted lines corresponding to the answer. (Find the pair of lines under the mark "B.")
4) Make a solid black mark between the dotted lines.

VI. BEFORE THE TEST

Common sense will help you find procedures to follow to get ready for an examination. Too many of us, however, overlook these sensible measures. Indeed, nervousness and fatigue have been found to be the most serious reasons why applicants fail to do their best on civil service tests. Here is a list of reminders:

- Begin your preparation early – Don't wait until the last minute to go scurrying around for books and materials or to find out what the position is all about.
- Prepare continuously – An hour a night for a week is better than an all-night cram session. This has been definitely established. What is more, a night a week for a month will return better dividends than crowding your study into a shorter period of time.
- Locate the place of the exam – You have been sent a notice telling you when and where to report for the examination. If the location is in a different town or otherwise unfamiliar to you, it would be well to inquire the best route and learn something about the building.
- Relax the night before the test – Allow your mind to rest. Do not study at all that night. Plan some mild recreation or diversion; then go to bed early and get a good night's sleep.
- Get up early enough to make a leisurely trip to the place for the test – This way unforeseen events, traffic snarls, unfamiliar buildings, etc. will not upset you.
- Dress comfortably – A written test is not a fashion show. You will be known by number and not by name, so wear something comfortable.

- Leave excess paraphernalia at home – Shopping bags and odd bundles will get in your way. You need bring only the items mentioned in the official notice you received; usually everything you need is provided. Do not bring reference books to the exam. They will only confuse those last minutes and be taken away from you when in the test room.
- Arrive somewhat ahead of time – If because of transportation schedules you must get there very early, bring a newspaper or magazine to take your mind off yourself while waiting.
- Locate the examination room – When you have found the proper room, you will be directed to the seat or part of the room where you will sit. Sometimes you are given a sheet of instructions to read while you are waiting. Do not fill out any forms until you are told to do so; just read them and be prepared.
- Relax and prepare to listen to the instructions
- If you have any physical problem that may keep you from doing your best, be sure to tell the test administrator. If you are sick or in poor health, you really cannot do your best on the exam. You can come back and take the test some other time.

VII. AT THE TEST

The day of the test is here and you have the test booklet in your hand. The temptation to get going is very strong. Caution! There is more to success than knowing the right answers. You must know how to identify your papers and understand variations in the type of short-answer question used in this particular examination. Follow these suggestions for maximum results from your efforts:

1) Cooperate with the monitor

The test administrator has a duty to create a situation in which you can be as much at ease as possible. He will give instructions, tell you when to begin, check to see that you are marking your answer sheet correctly, and so on. He is not there to guard you, although he will see that your competitors do not take unfair advantage. He wants to help you do your best.

2) Listen to all instructions

Don't jump the gun! Wait until you understand all directions. In most civil service tests you get more time than you need to answer the questions. So don't be in a hurry. Read each word of instructions until you clearly understand the meaning. Study the examples, listen to all announcements and follow directions. Ask questions if you do not understand what to do.

3) Identify your papers

Civil service exams are usually identified by number only. You will be assigned a number; you must not put your name on your test papers. Be sure to copy your number correctly. Since more than one exam may be given, copy your exact examination title.

4) Plan your time

Unless you are told that a test is a "speed" or "rate of work" test, speed itself is usually not important. Time enough to answer all the questions will be provided, but this does not mean that you have all day. An overall time limit has been set. Divide the total time (in minutes) by the number of questions to determine the approximate time you have for each question.

5) Do not linger over difficult questions

If you come across a difficult question, mark it with a paper clip (useful to have along) and come back to it when you have been through the booklet. One caution if you do this – be sure to skip a number on your answer sheet as well. Check often to be sure that you have not lost your place and that you are marking in the row numbered the same as the question you are answering.

6) Read the questions

Be sure you know what the question asks! Many capable people are unsuccessful because they failed to *read* the questions correctly.

7) Answer all questions

Unless you have been instructed that a penalty will be deducted for incorrect answers, it is better to guess than to omit a question.

8) Speed tests

It is often better NOT to guess on speed tests. It has been found that on timed tests people are tempted to spend the last few seconds before time is called in marking answers at random – without even reading them – in the hope of picking up a few extra points. To discourage this practice, the instructions may warn you that your score will be "corrected" for guessing. That is, a penalty will be applied. The incorrect answers will be deducted from the correct ones, or some other penalty formula will be used.

9) Review your answers

If you finish before time is called, go back to the questions you guessed or omitted to give them further thought. Review other answers if you have time.

10) Return your test materials

If you are ready to leave before others have finished or time is called, take ALL your materials to the monitor and leave quietly. Never take any test material with you. The monitor can discover whose papers are not complete, and taking a test booklet may be grounds for disqualification.

VIII. EXAMINATION TECHNIQUES

1) Read the general instructions carefully. These are usually printed on the first page of the exam booklet. As a rule, these instructions refer to the timing of the examination; the fact that you should not start work until the signal and must stop work at a signal, etc. If there are any *special* instructions, such as a choice of questions to be answered, make sure that you note this instruction carefully.

2) When you are ready to start work on the examination, that is as soon as the signal has been given, read the instructions to each question booklet, underline any key words or phrases, such as *least, best, outline, describe* and the like. In this way you will tend to answer as requested rather than discover on reviewing your paper that you *listed without describing*, that you selected the *worst* choice rather than the *best* choice, etc.

3) If the examination is of the objective or multiple-choice type – that is, each question will also give a series of possible answers: A, B, C or D, and you are called upon to select the best answer and write the letter next to that answer on your answer paper – it is advisable to start answering each question in turn. There may be anywhere from 50 to 100 such questions in the three or four hours allotted and you can see how much time would be taken if you read through all the questions before beginning to answer any. Furthermore, if you come across a question or group of questions which you know would be difficult to answer, it would undoubtedly affect your handling of all the other questions.

4) If the examination is of the essay type and contains but a few questions, it is a moot point as to whether you should read all the questions before starting to answer any one. Of course, if you are given a choice – say five out of seven and the like – then it is essential to read all the questions so you can eliminate the two that are most difficult. If, however, you are asked to answer all the questions, there may be danger in trying to answer the easiest one first because you may find that you will spend too much time on it. The best technique is to answer the first question, then proceed to the second, etc.

5) Time your answers. Before the exam begins, write down the time it started, then add the time allowed for the examination and write down the time it must be completed, then divide the time available somewhat as follows:
   - If 3-1/2 hours are allowed, that would be 210 minutes. If you have 80 objective-type questions, that would be an average of 2-1/2 minutes per question. Allow yourself no more than 2 minutes per question, or a total of 160 minutes, which will permit about 50 minutes to review.
   - If for the time allotment of 210 minutes there are 7 essay questions to answer, that would average about 30 minutes a question. Give yourself only 25 minutes per question so that you have about 35 minutes to review.

6) The most important instruction is to *read each question* and make sure you know what is wanted. The second most important instruction is to *time yourself properly* so that you answer every question. The third most important instruction is to *answer every question*. Guess if you have to but include something for each question. Remember that you will receive no credit for a blank and will probably receive some credit if you write something in answer to an essay question. If you guess a letter – say "B" for a multiple-choice question – you may have guessed right. If you leave a blank as an answer to a multiple-choice question, the examiners may respect your feelings but it will not add a point to your score. Some exams may penalize you for wrong answers, so in such cases *only*, you may not want to guess unless you have some basis for your answer.

7) Suggestions
   a. Objective-type questions
      1. Examine the question booklet for proper sequence of pages and questions
      2. Read all instructions carefully
      3. Skip any question which seems too difficult; return to it after all other questions have been answered
      4. Apportion your time properly; do not spend too much time on any single question or group of questions

5. Note and underline key words – *all, most, fewest, least, best, worst, same, opposite,* etc.
6. Pay particular attention to negatives
7. Note unusual option, e.g., unduly long, short, complex, different or similar in content to the body of the question
8. Observe the use of "hedging" words – *probably, may, most likely,* etc.
9. Make sure that your answer is put next to the same number as the question
10. Do not second-guess unless you have good reason to believe the second answer is definitely more correct
11. Cross out original answer if you decide another answer is more accurate; do not erase until you are ready to hand your paper in
12. Answer all questions; guess unless instructed otherwise
13. Leave time for review

b. Essay questions
   1. Read each question carefully
   2. Determine exactly what is wanted. Underline key words or phrases.
   3. Decide on outline or paragraph answer
   4. Include many different points and elements unless asked to develop any one or two points or elements
   5. Show impartiality by giving pros and cons unless directed to select one side only
   6. Make and write down any assumptions you find necessary to answer the questions
   7. Watch your English, grammar, punctuation and choice of words
   8. Time your answers; don't crowd material

8) Answering the essay question

Most essay questions can be answered by framing the specific response around several key words or ideas. Here are a few such key words or ideas:

M's: manpower, materials, methods, money, management
P's: purpose, program, policy, plan, procedure, practice, problems, pitfalls, personnel, public relations

   a. Six basic steps in handling problems:
      1. Preliminary plan and background development
      2. Collect information, data and facts
      3. Analyze and interpret information, data and facts
      4. Analyze and develop solutions as well as make recommendations
      5. Prepare report and sell recommendations
      6. Install recommendations and follow up effectiveness

   b. Pitfalls to avoid
      1. *Taking things for granted* – A statement of the situation does not necessarily imply that each of the elements is necessarily true; for example, a complaint may be invalid and biased so that all that can be taken for granted is that a complaint has been registered

2. *Considering only one side of a situation* – Wherever possible, indicate several alternatives and then point out the reasons you selected the best one
3. *Failing to indicate follow up* – Whenever your answer indicates action on your part, make certain that you will take proper follow-up action to see how successful your recommendations, procedures or actions turn out to be
4. *Taking too long in answering any single question* – Remember to time your answers properly

IX. AFTER THE TEST

Scoring procedures differ in detail among civil service jurisdictions although the general principles are the same. Whether the papers are hand-scored or graded by machine we have described, they are nearly always graded by number. That is, the person who marks the paper knows only the number – never the name – of the applicant. Not until all the papers have been graded will they be matched with names. If other tests, such as training and experience or oral interview ratings have been given, scores will be combined. Different parts of the examination usually have different weights. For example, the written test might count 60 percent of the final grade, and a rating of training and experience 40 percent. In many jurisdictions, veterans will have a certain number of points added to their grades.

After the final grade has been determined, the names are placed in grade order and an eligible list is established. There are various methods for resolving ties between those who get the same final grade – probably the most common is to place first the name of the person whose application was received first. Job offers are made from the eligible list in the order the names appear on it. You will be notified of your grade and your rank as soon as all these computations have been made. This will be done as rapidly as possible.

People who are found to meet the requirements in the announcement are called "eligibles." Their names are put on a list of eligible candidates. An eligible's chances of getting a job depend on how high he stands on this list and how fast agencies are filling jobs from the list.

When a job is to be filled from a list of eligibles, the agency asks for the names of people on the list of eligibles for that job. When the civil service commission receives this request, it sends to the agency the names of the three people highest on this list. Or, if the job to be filled has specialized requirements, the office sends the agency the names of the top three persons who meet these requirements from the general list.

The appointing officer makes a choice from among the three people whose names were sent to him. If the selected person accepts the appointment, the names of the others are put back on the list to be considered for future openings.

That is the rule in hiring from all kinds of eligible lists, whether they are for typist, carpenter, chemist, or something else. For every vacancy, the appointing officer has his choice of any one of the top three eligibles on the list. This explains why the person whose name is on top of the list sometimes does not get an appointment when some of the persons lower on the list do. If the appointing officer chooses the second or third eligible, the No. 1 eligible does not get a job at once, but stays on the list until he is appointed or the list is terminated.

X. HOW TO PASS THE INTERVIEW TEST

The examination for which you applied requires an oral interview test. You have already taken the written test and you are now being called for the interview test – the final part of the formal examination.

You may think that it is not possible to prepare for an interview test and that there are no procedures to follow during an interview. Our purpose is to point out some things you can do in advance that will help you and some good rules to follow and pitfalls to avoid while you are being interviewed.

What is an interview supposed to test?

The written examination is designed to test the technical knowledge and competence of the candidate; the oral is designed to evaluate intangible qualities, not readily measured otherwise, and to establish a list showing the relative fitness of each candidate – as measured against his competitors – for the position sought. Scoring is not on the basis of "right" and "wrong," but on a sliding scale of values ranging from "not passable" to "outstanding." As a matter of fact, it is possible to achieve a relatively low score without a single "incorrect" answer because of evident weakness in the qualities being measured.

Occasionally, an examination may consist entirely of an oral test – either an individual or a group oral. In such cases, information is sought concerning the technical knowledges and abilities of the candidate, since there has been no written examination for this purpose. More commonly, however, an oral test is used to supplement a written examination.

Who conducts interviews?

The composition of oral boards varies among different jurisdictions. In nearly all, a representative of the personnel department serves as chairman. One of the members of the board may be a representative of the department in which the candidate would work. In some cases, "outside experts" are used, and, frequently, a businessman or some other representative of the general public is asked to serve. Labor and management or other special groups may be represented. The aim is to secure the services of experts in the appropriate field.

However the board is composed, it is a good idea (and not at all improper or unethical) to ascertain in advance of the interview who the members are and what groups they represent. When you are introduced to them, you will have some idea of their backgrounds and interests, and at least you will not stutter and stammer over their names.

What should be done before the interview?

While knowledge about the board members is useful and takes some of the surprise element out of the interview, there is other preparation which is more substantive. It *is* possible to prepare for an oral interview – in several ways:

1) Keep a copy of your application and review it carefully before the interview

This may be the only document before the oral board, and the starting point of the interview. Know what education and experience you have listed there, and the sequence and dates of all of it. Sometimes the board will ask you to review the highlights of your experience for them; you should not have to hem and haw doing it.

2) Study the class specification and the examination announcement

Usually, the oral board has one or both of these to guide them. The qualities, characteristics or knowledges required by the position sought are stated in these documents. They offer valuable clues as to the nature of the oral interview. For example, if the job involves supervisory responsibilities, the announcement will usually indicate that knowledge of modern supervisory methods and the qualifications of the candidate as a supervisor will be tested. If so, you can expect such questions, frequently in the form of a hypothetical situation which you are expected to solve. NEVER go into an oral without knowledge of the duties and responsibilities of the job you seek.

3) Think through each qualification required

Try to visualize the kind of questions you would ask if you were a board member. How well could you answer them? Try especially to appraise your own knowledge and background in each area, *measured against the job sought*, and identify any areas in which you are weak. Be critical and realistic – do not flatter yourself.

4) Do some general reading in areas in which you feel you may be weak

For example, if the job involves supervision and your past experience has NOT, some general reading in supervisory methods and practices, particularly in the field of human relations, might be useful. Do NOT study agency procedures or detailed manuals. The oral board will be testing your understanding and capacity, not your memory.

5) Get a good night's sleep and watch your general health and mental attitude

You will want a clear head at the interview. Take care of a cold or any other minor ailment, and of course, no hangovers.

What should be done on the day of the interview?

Now comes the day of the interview itself. Give yourself plenty of time to get there. Plan to arrive somewhat ahead of the scheduled time, particularly if your appointment is in the fore part of the day. If a previous candidate fails to appear, the board might be ready for you a bit early. By early afternoon an oral board is almost invariably behind schedule if there are many candidates, and you may have to wait. Take along a book or magazine to read, or your application to review, but leave any extraneous material in the waiting room when you go in for your interview. In any event, relax and compose yourself.

The matter of dress is important. The board is forming impressions about you – from your experience, your manners, your attitude, and your appearance. Give your personal appearance careful attention. Dress your best, but not your flashiest. Choose conservative, appropriate clothing, and be sure it is immaculate. This is a business interview, and your appearance should indicate that you regard it as such. Besides, being well groomed and properly dressed will help boost your confidence.

Sooner or later, someone will call your name and escort you into the interview room. *This is it.* From here on you are on your own. It is too late for any more preparation. But remember, you asked for this opportunity to prove your fitness, and you are here because your request was granted.

What happens when you go in?

The usual sequence of events will be as follows: The clerk (who is often the board stenographer) will introduce you to the chairman of the oral board, who will introduce you to the other members of the board. Acknowledge the introductions before you sit down. Do not be surprised if you find a microphone facing you or a stenotypist sitting by. Oral interviews are usually recorded in the event of an appeal or other review.

Usually the chairman of the board will open the interview by reviewing the highlights of your education and work experience from your application – primarily for the benefit of the other members of the board, as well as to get the material into the record. Do not interrupt or comment unless there is an error or significant misinterpretation; if that is the case, do not hesitate. But do not quibble about insignificant matters. Also, he will usually ask you some question about your education, experience or your present job – partly to get you to start talking and to establish the interviewing "rapport." He may start the actual questioning, or turn it over to one of the other members. Frequently, each member undertakes the questioning on a particular area, one in which he is perhaps most competent, so you can expect each member to participate in the examination. Because time is limited, you may also expect some rather abrupt switches in the direction the questioning takes, so do not be upset by it. Normally, a board member will not pursue a single line of questioning unless he discovers a particular strength or weakness.

After each member has participated, the chairman will usually ask whether any member has any further questions, then will ask you if you have anything you wish to add. Unless you are expecting this question, it may floor you. Worse, it may start you off on an extended, extemporaneous speech. The board is not usually seeking more information. The question is principally to offer you a last opportunity to present further qualifications or to indicate that you have nothing to add. So, if you feel that a significant qualification or characteristic has been overlooked, it is proper to point it out in a sentence or so. Do not compliment the board on the thoroughness of their examination – they have been sketchy, and you know it. If you wish, merely say, "No thank you, I have nothing further to add." This is a point where you can "talk yourself out" of a good impression or fail to present an important bit of information. Remember, *you close the interview yourself.*

The chairman will then say, "That is all, Mr. _____, thank you." Do not be startled; the interview is over, and quicker than you think. Thank him, gather your belongings and take your leave. Save your sigh of relief for the other side of the door.

How to put your best foot forward

Throughout this entire process, you may feel that the board individually and collectively is trying to pierce your defenses, seek out your hidden weaknesses and embarrass and confuse you. Actually, this is not true. They are obliged to make an appraisal of your qualifications for the job you are seeking, and they want to see you in your best light. Remember, they must interview all candidates and a non-cooperative candidate may become a failure in spite of their best efforts to bring out his qualifications. Here are 15 suggestions that will help you:

1) Be natural – Keep your attitude confident, not cocky

If you are not confident that you can do the job, do not expect the board to be. Do not apologize for your weaknesses, try to bring out your strong points. The board is interested in a positive, not negative, presentation. Cockiness will antagonize any board member and make him wonder if you are covering up a weakness by a false show of strength.

2) Get comfortable, but don't lounge or sprawl

Sit erectly but not stiffly. A careless posture may lead the board to conclude that you are careless in other things, or at least that you are not impressed by the importance of the occasion. Either conclusion is natural, even if incorrect. Do not fuss with your clothing, a pencil or an ashtray. Your hands may occasionally be useful to emphasize a point; do not let them become a point of distraction.

3) Do not wisecrack or make small talk

This is a serious situation, and your attitude should show that you consider it as such. Further, the time of the board is limited – they do not want to waste it, and neither should you.

4) Do not exaggerate your experience or abilities
In the first place, from information in the application or other interviews and sources, the board may know more about you than you think. Secondly, you probably will not get away with it. An experienced board is rather adept at spotting such a situation, so do not take the chance.

5) If you know a board member, do not make a point of it, yet do not hide it
Certainly you are not fooling him, and probably not the other members of the board. Do not try to take advantage of your acquaintanceship – it will probably do you little good.

6) Do not dominate the interview
Let the board do that. They will give you the clues – do not assume that you have to do all the talking. Realize that the board has a number of questions to ask you, and do not try to take up all the interview time by showing off your extensive knowledge of the answer to the first one.

7) Be attentive
You only have 20 minutes or so, and you should keep your attention at its sharpest throughout. When a member is addressing a problem or question to you, give him your undivided attention. Address your reply principally to him, but do not exclude the other board members.

8) Do not interrupt
A board member may be stating a problem for you to analyze. He will ask you a question when the time comes. Let him state the problem, and wait for the question.

9) Make sure you understand the question
Do not try to answer until you are sure what the question is. If it is not clear, restate it in your own words or ask the board member to clarify it for you. However, do not haggle about minor elements.

10) Reply promptly but not hastily
A common entry on oral board rating sheets is "candidate responded readily," or "candidate hesitated in replies." Respond as promptly and quickly as you can, but do not jump to a hasty, ill-considered answer.

11) Do not be peremptory in your answers
A brief answer is proper – but do not fire your answer back. That is a losing game from your point of view. The board member can probably ask questions much faster than you can answer them.

12) Do not try to create the answer you think the board member wants
He is interested in what kind of mind you have and how it works – not in playing games. Furthermore, he can usually spot this practice and will actually grade you down on it.

13) Do not switch sides in your reply merely to agree with a board member
Frequently, a member will take a contrary position merely to draw you out and to see if you are willing and able to defend your point of view. Do not start a debate, yet do not surrender a good position. If a position is worth taking, it is worth defending.

14) Do not be afraid to admit an error in judgment if you are shown to be wrong

The board knows that you are forced to reply without any opportunity for careful consideration. Your answer may be demonstrably wrong. If so, admit it and get on with the interview.

15) Do not dwell at length on your present job

The opening question may relate to your present assignment. Answer the question but do not go into an extended discussion. You are being examined for a *new* job, not your present one. As a matter of fact, try to phrase ALL your answers in terms of the job for which you are being examined.

Basis of Rating

Probably you will forget most of these "do's" and "don'ts" when you walk into the oral interview room. Even remembering them all will not ensure you a passing grade. Perhaps you did not have the qualifications in the first place. But remembering them will help you to put your best foot forward, without treading on the toes of the board members.

Rumor and popular opinion to the contrary notwithstanding, an oral board wants you to make the best appearance possible. They know you are under pressure – but they also want to see how you respond to it as a guide to what your reaction would be under the pressures of the job you seek. They will be influenced by the degree of poise you display, the personal traits you show and the manner in which you respond.

ABOUT THIS BOOK

This book contains tests divided into Examination Sections. Go through each test, answering every question in the margin. We have also attached a sample answer sheet at the back of the book that can be removed and used. At the end of each test look at the answer key and check your answers. On the ones you got wrong, look at the right answer choice and learn. Do not fill in the answers first. Do not memorize the questions and answers, but understand the answer and principles involved. On your test, the questions will likely be different from the samples. Questions are changed and new ones added. If you understand these past questions you should have success with any changes that arise. Tests may consist of several types of questions. We have additional books on each subject should more study be advisable or necessary for you. Finally, the more you study, the better prepared you will be. This book is intended to be the last thing you study before you walk into the examination room. Prior study of relevant texts is also recommended. NLC publishes some of these in our Fundamental Series. Knowledge and good sense are important factors in passing your exam. Good luck also helps. So now study this Passbook, absorb the material contained within and take that knowledge into the examination. Then do your best to pass that exam.

EXAMINATION SECTION

EXAMINATION SECTION
TEST 1

DIRECTIONS: Each question or incomplete statement is followed by several suggested answers or completions. Select the one that BEST answers the question or completes the statement. *PRINT THE LETTER OF THE CORRECT ANSWER IN THE SPACE AT THE RIGHT.*

Questions 1-4.

DIRECTIONS: Questions 1 through 4 are to be answered on the basis of the following passage.

Those engaged in the exercise of First Amendment rights by pickets, marches, parades, and open-air assemblies are not exempted from obeying valid local traffic ordinances. In a recent pronouncement, Mr. Justice Baxter, speaking for the Supreme Court, wrote:

The rights of free speech and assembly, while fundamental to our democratic society, still do not mean that everyone with opinions or beliefs to express may address a group at any public place and at any time. The constitutional guarantee of liberty implies the existence of an organized society maintaining public order, without which liberty itself would be lost in the excesses of anarchy. The control of travel on the streets is a clear example of governmental responsibility to insure this necessary order. A restriction in that relation, designed to promote the public convenience in the interest of all, and not susceptible to abuses of discriminatory application, cannot be disregarded by the attempted exercise of some civil rights which, in other circumstances, would be entitled to protection. One would not be justified in ignoring the familiar red light because this was thought to be a means of social protest. Governmental authorities have the duty and responsibility to keep their streets open and available for movement. A group of demonstrators could not insist upon the right to cordon off a street, or entrance to a public or private building, and allow no one to pass who did not agree to listen to their exhortations.

1. Which of the following statements BEST reflects Mr. Justice Baxter's view of the relationship between liberty and public order?   1.____

    A. Public order cannot exist without liberty.
    B. Liberty cannot exist without public order.
    C. The existence of liberty undermines the existence of public order.
    D. The maintenance of public order insures the existence of liberty.

2. According to the above passage, local traffic ordinances result from   2.____

    A. governmental limitations on individual liberty
    B. governmental responsibility to insure public order
    C. majority rule as determined by democratic procedures
    D. restrictions on expression of dissent

3. The foregoing passage suggests that government would be acting IMPROPERLY if a local traffic ordinance   3.____

    A. was enforced in a discriminatory manner
    B. resulted in public inconvenience

1

C. violated the right of free speech and assembly
D. was not essential to public order

4. Of the following, the MOST appropriate title for the above passage is:

   A. THE RIGHTS OF FREE SPEECH AND ASSEMBLY
   B. ENFORCEMENT OF LOCAL TRAFFIC ORDINANCES
   C. FIRST AMENDMENT RIGHTS AND LOCAL TRAFFIC ORDINANCES
   D. LIBERTY AND ANARCHY

Questions 5-8.

DIRECTIONS: Questions 5 through 8 are to be answered on the basis of the following passage.

On November 8, 1976, the Supreme Court refused to block the payment of Medicaid funds for elective abortions. The Court's action means that a new Federal statute that bars the use of Federal funds for abortions unless abortion is necessary to save the life of the mother will not go into effect for many months, if at all.

A Federal District Court in Brooklyn ruled the following month that the statute was unconstitutional and ordered that Federal reimbursement for the costs of abortions continue on the same basis as reimbursements for the costs of pregnancy and childbirth-related services.

Technically, what the Court did today was to deny a request by Senator Howard Ramsdell and others for a stay blocking enforcement of the District Court order pending appeal. The Court's action was a victory for New York City. The City's Health and Hospitals Corporation initiated one of the two lawsuits challenging the new statute that led to the District Court's decision. The Corporation also opposed the request for a Supreme Court stay of that decision, telling the Court in a memorandum that a stay would subject the Corporation to a grave and irreparable injury."

5. According to the above passage, it would be CORRECT to state that the Health and Hospitals Corporation

   A. joined Senator Ramsdell in his request for a stay
   B. opposed the statute which limited reimbursement for the cost of abortions
   C. claimed that it would experience a loss if the District Court order was enforced
   D. appealed the District Court decision

6. The above passage indicates that the Supreme Court acted in DIRECT response to

   A. a lawsuit initiated by the Health and Hospitals Corporation
   B. a ruling by a Federal District Court
   C. a request for a stay
   D. the passage of a new Federal statute

7. According to the above passage, it would be CORRECT to state that the Supreme Court

   A. blocked enforcement of the District Court order
   B. refused a request for a stay to block enforcement of the Federal statute
   C. ruled that the new Federal statute was unconstitutional
   D. permitted payment of Federal funds for abortion to continue

8. Following are three statements concerning abortion that might be correct:
    I. Abortion costs are no longer to be Federally reimbursed on the same basis as those for pregnancy and childbirth
    II. Federal funds have not been available for abortions except to save the life of the mother
    III. Medicaid has paid for elective abortions in the past

    According to the passage given above, which of the following CORRECTLY classifies the above statements into those that are true and those that are not true?

    A. I is true, but II and III are not.
    B. I and III are true, but II is not.
    C. I and II are true, but III is not.
    D. III is true, but I and II are not.

9. A legal memorandum will often include the following six sections:
    I. Conclusions
    II. Issues
    III. Analysis
    IV. Facts
    V. Unknowns
    VI. Counter-analysis

    Which of the following choices lists these sections in the sequence that is generally MOST appropriate for a legal memorandum?

    A. III, VI, IV, V, II, I
    B. IV, II, III, VI, I, V
    C. V, II, IV, III, VI, I
    D. II, IV, V, III, I, VI

Questions 10-13.

DIRECTIONS: Questions 10 through 13 consist of two sentences each. The sentences deal with the use of court opinions and cases in the writing of legal memoranda. Select answer
    A. if only sentence I is correct
    B. if only sentence II is correct
    C. if both sentences are correct
    D. if neither sentence is correct

10. I. State the issues in the case as narrowly and precisely as possible.
    II. Quote frequently and at great length from the court opinions.

11. I. Describe briefly the issues in the case that are not related to your problem.
    II. Do not mention discrepancies between the facts of the case and the facts of your problem.

12. I. Do not refer to the holding or ruling in the case if it is harmful to your client.
    II. If the holding or ruling in the case is beneficial to your client, try to show that the facts of your problem are analogous to the facts of the case.

13. I. After stating your position concerning the issues and facts, present the opposite viewpoint as effectively as you can.
    II. Avoid stating your own opinions or conclusions concerning the applicability of the case.

14. Column V lists four publications in the legal field. Column W contains descriptions of basic subject matter of legal publications.
Select the one of the following choices which BEST matches the publications in Column V with the subject matter in Column W.

Column V	Column W
I. Harvard Law Review	1. Law
II. Supreme Court Reporter	2. Commentary on law
III. McKinney's Consolidated Laws of New York	3. Combination of law and commentary
IV. The Criminal Law Reporter	

    A. I-3; II-1; III-2; IV-3
    B. I-2; II-3; III-2; IV-3
    C. I-2; II-1; III-3; IV-3
    D. I-2; II-3; III-3; IV-1

15. Tickler systems are used in many legal offices for scheduling and calendar control. Of the following, the LEAST common use of a tickler system is to

    A. keep papers filed in such a way that they may easily be retrieved
    B. arrange for the appearance of witnesses when they will be needed
    C. remind lawyers when certain papers are due
    D. arrange for the gathering of certain types of evidence

KEY (CORRECT ANSWERS)

1. B
2. B
3. A
4. C
5. B

6. C
7. D
8. D
9. B
10. A

11. D
12. B
13. A
14. C
15. A

TEST 2

DIRECTIONS: Each question or incomplete statement is followed by several suggested answers or completions. Select the one that BEST answers the question or completes the statement. *PRINT THE LETTER OF THE CORRECT ANSWER IN THE SPACE AT THE RIGHT.*

1. Studying the legislative history of a statute by reading the transcript of the hearings that were held on that subject is useful to the legal researcher PRIMARILY because it

   A. is informative of the manner in which laws are enacted
   B. helps him to understand the intent of the statute
   C. provides leads to statutes on the same subject
   D. clarifies the meaning of other statutes

1.____

2. Following are three statements concerning legal research that might be correct:
   I. The researcher may begin with a particular premise and, in researching it, may discover an entirely new approach to the problem
   II. When the researcher has located a relevant statute, it is not necessary to read court opinions interpreting or applying this statute
   III. A statute which is related to, but not the same as, the point being researched may have notes which will refer the researcher to more relevant cases

   Which of the following ACCURATELY classifies the above statements into those which are correct and those which are not?

   A. II and III are correct, but I is not.
   B. I and III are correct, but II is not.
   C. I and II are correct, but III is not.
   D. I, II, and III are all correct.

2.____

3. Of the following, the FIRST action a legal researcher should take in order to locate the laws relevant to a case is to

   A. search the index of a law book
   B. read statutes on similar subjects to discover pertinent annotations
   C. read a legal digest to become familiar with the law on the subject
   D. prepare a list of descriptive words applicable to the facts of the case

3.____

4. Which of the following is the BEST source for a legal researcher to consult in order to find historical data, cross-references, and case excerpts on cases, statutes, and regulations?

   A. Annotations   B. Digests
   C. Hornbooks   D. Casebooks

4.____

Questions 5-8.

DIRECTIONS: Each of Questions 5 through 8 contains two sentences concerning criminal law. Some of the sentences contain errors in English grammar or usage. A sentence does not contain an error simply because it could be written in a different manner. For each question, choose answer
   A. if only sentence I is correct
   B. if only sentence II is correct
   C. if both sentences are correct
   D. if neither sentence is correct

5. I. Limiting the term *property* to tangible property, in the criminal mischief setting, accords with prior case law holding that only tangible property came within the purview of the offense of malicious mischief.
    II. Thus, a person who intentionally destroys the property of another, but under an honest belief that he has title to such property, cannot be convicted of criminal mischief under the Revised Penal Law.

6. I. Very early in it's history, New York enacted statutes from time to time punishing, either as a felony or as a misdemeanor, malicious injuries to various kinds of property: piers, booms, dams, bridges, etc.
    II. The application of the statute is necessarily restricted to trespassory takings with larcenous intent: namely with intent permanently or virtually permanently to *appropriate* property or *deprive* the owner of its use.

7. I. Since the former Penal Law did not define the instruments of forgery in a general fashion, its crime of forgery was held to be narrower than the common law offense in this respect and to embrace only those instruments explicitly specified in the substantive provisions.
    II. After entering the barn through an open door for the purpose of stealing, it was closed by the defendants.

8. I. The use of fire or explosives to destroy tangible property is proscribed by the criminal mischief provisions of the Revised Penal Law.
    II. The defendant's taking of a taxicab for the immediate purpose of affecting his escape did not constitute grand larceny

Questions 9-13.

DIRECTIONS: Questions 9 through 13 are to be answered SOLELY on the basis of the following passage.

The law is quite clear that evidence obtained in violation of Section 605 of the Federal Communications Act is not admissible in federal court. However, the law as to the admissibility of evidence in state court is far from clear. Had the Supreme Court of the United States made the wiretap exclusionary rule applicable to the states, such confusion would not exist.

In the case of Alton v. Texas, the Supreme Court was called upon to determine whether wiretapping by state and local officers came within the proscription of the federal statute and, if so, whether Section 605 required the same remedies for its vindication in state courts. In answer to the first question, Mr. Justice Minton, speaking for the court, flatly stated that Section 605 made it a federal crime for anyone to intercept telephone messages and divulge what he learned. The court went on to say that a state officer who testified in state court concerning the existence, contents, substance, purport, effect or meaning of an intercepted conversation violated the federal law and committed a criminal act. In regard to the second question, however, the Supreme Court felt constrained by due regard for federal-state relations to answer in the negative. Mr. Justice Minton stated that the court would not presume, in the absence of a clear manifestation of congressional intent, that Congress intended to supersede state rules of evidence.

Because the Supreme Court refused to apply the exclusionary rule to wiretap evidence that was being used in state courts, the states respectively made this decision for themselves. According to hearings held before a congressional committee in 1975, six states authorize wiretapping by statute, 33 states impose total bans on wiretapping, and 11 states have no definite statute on the subject. For examples of extremes, a statute in Pennsylvania will be compared with a statute in New York.

The Pennsylvania statute provides that no communications by telephone or telegraph can be intercepted without permission of both parties. It also specifically prohibits such interception by public officials and provides that evidence obtained cannot be used in court.

The lawmakers in New York, recognizing the need for legal wiretapping, authorized wiretapping by statute. A New York law authorizes the issuance of an ex parte order upon oath or affirmation for limited wiretapping. The aim of the New York law is to allow court-ordered wiretapping and to encourage the testimony of state officers concerning such wiretapping in court. The New York law was found to be constitutional by the New York State Supreme Court in 1975. Other states, including Oregon, Maryland, Nevada, and Massachusetts, enacted similar laws which authorize court-ordered wiretapping.

To add to this legal disarray, the vast majority of the states, including New Jersey and New York, permit wiretapping evidence to be received in court even though obtained in violation of the state laws and of Section 605 of the Federal act. However, some states such as Rhode Island have enacted statutory exclusionary rules which provide that illegally procured wiretap evidence is incompetent in civil as well as criminal actions.

9. According to the above passage, a state officer who testifies in New York State court concerning the contents of a conversation he overheard through a court-ordered wiretap is in violation of _____ law.

    A. state law but not federal
    B. federal law but not state
    C. federal law and state
    D. neither federal nor state

10. According to the above passage, which of the following statements concerning states statutes on wiretapping is CORRECT?

    A. The number of states that impose total bans on wiretapping is three times as great as the number of states with no definite statute on wiretapping.
    B. The number of states having no definite statute on wiretapping is more than twice the number of states authorizing wiretapping.
    C. The number of states which authorize wiretapping by statute and the number of states having no definite statute on wiretapping exceed the number of states imposing total bans on wiretapping.
    D. More states authorize wiretapping by statute than impose total bans on wiretapping.

11. Following are three statements concerning wiretapping that might be valid:
    I. In Pennsylvania, only public officials may legally intercept telephone communications
    II. In Rhode Island, evidence obtained through an illegal wiretap is incompetent in criminal, but not civil, actions
    III. Neither Massachusetts nor Pennsylvania authorizes wiretapping by public officials

    According to the above passage, which of the following CORRECTLY classifies these statements into those that are valid and those that are not?

    A. I is valid, but II and III are not.
    B. II is valid, but I and III are not.
    C. II and III are valid, but I is not.
    D. None of the statements is valid.

12. According to the foregoing passage, evidence obtained in violation of Section 605 of the Federal Communications Act is inadmissible in

    A. federal court but not in any state courts
    B. federal court and all state courts
    C. all state courts but not in federal court
    D. federal court and some state courts

13. In regard to state rules of evidence, Mr. Justice Minton expressed the Court's opinion that Congress

    A. intended to supersede state rules of evidence, as manifested by Section 605 of the Federal Communications Act
    B. assumed that federal statutes would govern state rules of evidence in all wiretap cases
    C. left unclear whether it intended to supersede state rules of evidence
    D. precluded itself from superseding state rules of evidence through its regard for federal-state relations

14. You begin to ask follow-up questions of a witness who has given a statement. The witness starts to digress before answering an important question satisfactorily.
    In this situation, the BEST of the following steps is to

    A. guide the interview by suggesting answers to questions as they are asked
    B. ask questions which can be answered only with a simple *yes* or *no*
    C. construct questions as precisely as possible
    D. tell the witness to keep his answers brief

15. During an interview with a client, you have occasion to refer to a matter which is described in the legal profession by a technical term.
    Of the following, it would generally be MOST appropriate for you to

    A. discuss the underlying legal concept in detail
    B. avoid the subject since it is too complicated
    C. ask the client if he is familiar with the technical term
    D. describe the matter in everyday language

KEY (CORRECT ANSWERS)

1. B
2. B
3. D
4. A
5. C

6. B
7. A
8. A
9. B
10. A

11. D
12. D
13. C
14. C
15. D

EXAMINATION SECTION
TEST 1

DIRECTIONS: Each question or incomplete statement is followed by several suggested answers or completions. Select the one that BEST answers the question or completes the statement. *PRINT THE LETTER OF THE CORRECT ANSWER IN THE SPACE AT THE RIGHT.*

Questions 1-4.

DIRECTIONS: Questions 1 through 4 consist of sentences concerning criminal law. Some of the sentences contain errors in English grammar or usage, punctuation, spelling or capitalization. A sentence does not contain an error simply because it could be written in a different manner. Choose answer
- A. if the sentence contains an error in English grammar or usage
- B. if the sentence contains an error in punctuation
- C. if the sentence contains an error in spelling or capitalization
- D. if the sentence does not contain any errors

1. The severity of the sentence prescribed by contemporary statutes - including both the former and the revised New York Penal Laws - do not depend on what crime was intended by the offender.   1.____

2. It is generally recognized that two defects in the early law of attempt played a part in the birth of burglary: (1) immunity from prosecution for conduct short of the last act before completion of the crime, and (2) the relatively minor penalty imposed for an attempt (it being a common law misdemeanor) vis-a-vis the completed offense.   2.____

3. The first sentence of the statute is applicable to employees who enter their place of employment, invited guests, and all other persons who have an express or implied license or privilege to enter the premises.   3.____

4. Contemporary criminal codes in the United States generally divide burglary into various degrees, differentiating the categories according to place, time and other attendent circumstances.   4.____

Questions 5-8.

DIRECTIONS: Questions 5 through 8 are to be answered SOLELY on the basis of the following passage.

The difficulty experienced in determining which party has the burden of proving payment or non-payment is due largely to a tack of consistency between the rules of pleading and the rules of proof. In some cases, a plaintiff is obligated by a rule of pleading to allege non-payment on his complaint, yet is not obligated to prove non-payment on the trial. An action upon a contract for the payment of money will serve as an illustration. In such a case, the plaintiff must allege non-payment in his complaint, but the burden of proving payment on the trial is upon the defendant. An important and frequently cited case on this problem is Conkling v. Weatherwax. In that case, the action was brought to establish and enforce a legacy as a lien upon real property. The defendant alleged in her answer that the legacy had been paid. There was no witness competent to testify for the plaintiff to show that the legacy had not been paid. Therefore, the question of the burden of proof became of primary importance since, if the plaintiff had the burden of proving non-payment, she must fail in her action; whereas, if the burden of proof was on the defendant to prove payment, the plaintiff might win. The Court of Appeals held that the burden of proof was on the plaintiff. In the course of his opinion, Judge Vann attempted to harmonize the conflicting cases on this subject, and for that purpose formulated three rules. These rules have been construed and applied to numerous subsequent cases. As so construed and applied, these may be summarized as follows:

Rule 1: In an action upon a contract for the payment of money only, where the complaint does not allege a balance due over and above all payments made, the plaintiff must allege nonpayment in his complaint, but the burden of proving payment is upon the defendant. In such a case, payment is an affirmative defense which the defendant must plead in his answer. If the defendant fails to plead payment, but pleads a general denial instead, he will not be permitted to introduce evidence of payment.

Rule 2: Where the complaint sets forth a balance in excess of all payments, owing to the structure of the pleading, burden is upon the plaintiff to prove his allegation. In this case, the defendant is not required to plead payment as a defense in his answer but may introduce evidence of payment under a general denial.

Rule 3: When the action is not upon contract for the payment of money, but is upon an obligation created by operation of law, or is for the enforcement of a lien where non-payment of the amount secured is part of the cause of action, it is necessary both to allege and prove the fact of nonpayment.

5. In the above passage, the case of Conkling v. Weatherwax was cited PRIMARILY to illustrate

    A. a case where the burden of proof was on the defendant to prove payment
    B. how the question of the burden of proof can affect the outcome of a case
    C. the effect of a legacy as a lien upon real property
    D. how conflicting cases concerning the burden of proof were harmonized

6. According to the above passage, the pleading of payment is a defense in

    A. Rule 1, but not Rules 2 and 3
    B. Rule 2, but not Rules 1 and 3
    C. Rules 1 and 3, but not Rule 2
    D. Rules 2 and 3, but not Rule 1

7. The facts in Conkling v. Weatherwax closely resemble the conditions described in Rule

    A. 1
    B. 2
    C. 3
    D. none of the rules

8. The major topic of the above passage may BEST be described as

    A. determining the ownership of property
    B. providing a legal definition
    C. placing the burden of proof
    D. formulating rules for deciding cases

Questions 9-12.

DIRECTIONS: Questions 9 through 12 consist of six sentences which can be arranged in a logical sequence. For each question, select the choice which places the numbered sentences in the MOST logical sequence.

9. I. The burden of proof as to each issue is determined before trial and remains upon the same party throughout the trial.
    II. The jury is at liberty to believe one witness testimony as against a number of contradictory witnesses.
    III. In a civil case, the party bearing the burden of proof is required to prove his contention by a fair preponderance of the evidence.
    IV. However, it must be noted that a fair preponderance of evidence does not necessarily mean a greater number of witnesses.
    V. The burden of proof is the burden which rests upon one of the parties to an action to persuade the trier of the facts, generally the jury, that a proposition he asserts is true.
    VI. If the evidence is equally balanced, or if it leaves the jury in such doubt as to be unable to decide the controversy either way, judgment must be given against the party upon whom the burden of proof rests.

    The CORRECT sequence is:

    A. III, II, V, IV, I, VI
    B. I, II, VI, V, III, IV
    C. III, IV, V, I, II, VI
    D. V, I, III, VI, IV, II

10. I. If a parent is without assets and is unemployed, he cannot be convicted of the crime of non-support of a child.
    II. The term *sufficient ability* has been held to mean sufficient financial ability.
    III. It does not matter if his unemployment is by choice or unavoidable circumstances.
    IV. If he fails to take any steps at all, he may be liable to prosecution for endangering the welfare of a child.
    V. Under the penal law, a parent is responsible for the support of his minor child only if the parent is of sufficient ability.
    VI. An indigent parent may meet his obligation by borrowing money or by seeking aid under the provisions of the Social Welfare Law.

    The CORRECT sequence is:

    A. VI, I, V, III, II, IV
    B. I, III, V, II, IV, VI
    C. V, II, I, III, VI, IV
    D. I, VI, IV, V, II, III

11.
I. Consider, for example, the case of a rabble rouser who urges a group of twenty people to go out and break the windows of a nearby factory.
II. Therefore, the law fills the indicated gap with the crime of *inciting to riot*.
III. A person is considered guilty of inciting to riot when he urges ten or more persons to engage in tumultuous and violent conduct of a kind likely to create public alarm.
IV. However, if he has not obtained the cooperation of at least four people, he cannot be charged with unlawful assembly.
V. The charge of inciting to riot was added to the law to cover types of conduct which cannot be classified as either the crime of *riot* or the crime of *unlawful* assembly.
VI. If he acquires the acquiescence of at least four of them, he is guilty of unlawful assembly even if the project does not materialize.

The CORRECT sequence is:

A. III, V, I, VI, IV, II
B. V, I, IV, VI, II, III
C. III, IV, I, V, II, VI
D. V, I, IV, VI, III, II

12.
I. If, however, the rebuttal evidence presents an issue of credibility, it is for the jury to determine whether the presumption has, in fact, been destroyed.
II. Once sufficient evidence to the contrary is introduced, the presumption disappears from the trial.
III. The effect of a presumption is to place the burden upon the adversary to come forward with evidence to rebut the presumption.
IV. When a presumption is overcome and ceases to exist in the case, the fact or facts which gave rise to the presumption still remain.
V. Whether a presumption has been overcome is ordinarily a question for the court.
VI. Such information may furnish a basis for a logical inference.

The CORRECT sequence is:

A. IV, VI, II, V, I, III
B. III, II, V, I, IV, VI
C. V, III, VI, IV, II, I
D. V, IV, I, II, VI, III

13. In order to obtain an accurate statement from a person who has witnessed a crime, it is BEST to question the witness

A. as soon as possible after the crime was committed
B. after the witness has discussed the crime with other witnesses
C. after the witness has had sufficient time to reflect on events and formulate a logical statement
D. after the witness has been advised that he is obligated to tell the whole truth

14. A young woman was stabbed in the hand in her home by her estranged boyfriend. Her mother and two sisters were at home at the time.
Of the following, it would generally be BEST to interview the young woman in the presence of

A. her mother only
B. all members of her immediate family
C. members of the family who actually observed the crime
D. the official authorities

15. The one of the following which is NOT effective in obtaining complete testimony from a witness during an interview is to

    A. ask questions in chronological order
    B. permit the witness to structure the interview
    C. make sure you fully understand the response to each question
    D. review questions to be asked beforehand

KEY (CORRECT ANSWERS)

1. A	6. A
2. D	7. C
3. D	8. C
4. C	9. D
5. B	10. C

11. A
12. B
13. A
14. D
15. B

TEST 2

DIRECTIONS: Each question or incomplete statement is followed by several suggested answers or completions. Select the one that BEST answers the question or completes the statement. *PRINT THE LETTER OF THE CORRECT ANSWER IN THE SPACE AT THE RIGHT.*

1. You are conducting an initial interview with a witness who expresses reluctance, even hostility, to being questioned. You feel it would be helpful to take some notes during the interview.
   In this situation, it would be BEST to

   A. put off note-taking until a follow-up interview and concentrate on establishing rapport with the witness
   B. explain the necessity of note-taking and proceed to take notes during the interview
   C. make notes from memory after the witness has left
   D. take notes, but as unobtrusively as possible

2. An assistant is starting an interview with an elderly man who was the victim of a robbery. The man begins by mentioning his minor aches and pains. The aide immediately changes the subject to the robbery.
   This action by the aide should GENERALLY be considered

   A. *proper* chiefly because it speeds up the interviewing process
   B. *improper* chiefly because the man is likely to become confused as to what information is really important
   C. *proper* chiefly because the man is likely to be impressed with the aide's interest in the crime
   D. *improper* chiefly because an opportunity for gaining pertinent information may be lost

3. You are interviewing the owner of a stolen car about facts relating to the robbery. After completing his statement, the car owner suddenly states that some of the details he has just related are not correct. You realize that this change might be significant.
   Of the following, it would be BEST for you to

   A. ask the owner what other details he may have given incorrectly
   B. make a note of the discrepancy for discussion at a later date
   C. repeat your questioning on the details that were misstated until you have covered that area completely
   D. explain to the owner that because of his change of testimony, you will have to repeat the entire interview

4. You are interviewing a client who has just been assaulted. He has trouble collecting his thoughts and telling his story coherently.
   Which of the following represents the MOST effective method of questioning under these circumstances?

   A. Ask questions which structure the client's story chronologically into units, each with a beginning, middle, and end.
   B. Ask several questions at a time to structure the interview.

C. Ask open-ended questions which allow the client to respond in a variety of ways.
D. Begin the interview with several detailed questions in order to focus the client's attention on the situation.

5. Following are two statements that might be correct concerning the relationship with clients:
   I. When practical the client should be encouraged to take some steps on his own behalf to aid the office in handling his case
   II. The client should be told what steps the office proposes to take on his behalf

   Which of the following CORRECTLY classifies the above statements?

   A. Statement I is generally correct, but Statement II is not.
   B. Statement II is generally correct, but Statement I is not.
   C. Both statements are generally correct.
   D. Neither statement is generally correct.

6. You are in the District Attorney's office interviewing an elderly female victim of an assault in order to prepare a list of charges.
   The one of the following which would be MOST important in determining all the facts is

   A. creating a close, cooperative working relationship with the victim
   B. establishing your authority at the beginning of the interview
   C. maintaining a relaxed atmosphere during the interview
   D. having access to the particular statutes which might apply to this case

7. A client is critical of the way he has been treated by government agencies in the past. A paralegal aide interviewing him defends the overall performance of government employees.
   This reaction by the aide is GENERALLY

   A. *appropriate;* the aide has an obligation to defend fellow workers in government service when such defense is justified
   B. *inappropriate;* the aide should remain neutral rather than volunteer his personal opinions
   C. *appropriate;* the aide should honestly express his personal opinions in such circumstances unless it is likely to provoke antagonism
   D. *inappropriate;* the aide should agree with the client's comments to help establish a greater rapport with him

Questions 8-11.

DIRECTIONS: Questions 8 through 11 are to be answered SOLELY on the basis of the following passage.

A person may use physical force upon another person when and to the extent he reasonably believes such to be necessary to defend himself or a third person from what he reasonably believes to be the use or imminent use of unlawful physical force by such other person, unless (a) the latter's conduct was provoked by the actor himself with intent to cause physical injury to another person, or (b) the actor was the initial aggressor; or (c) the physical force involved is the product of a combat by agreement not specifically authorized by law.

A person may not use deadly physical force upon another person under the circumstances specified above unless: (a) he reasonably believes that such other person is using or is about to use deadly physical force. Even in such case, however, the actor may not use deadly physical force if he knows he can with complete safety as to himself and others avoid the necessity of doing so by retreating, except that he is under no duty to retreat if he is in his dwelling and is not the initial aggressor; or (b) he reasonably believes that such other person is committing or attempting to commit a kidnapping, forcible rape, or forcible sodomy.

8. Jones and Smith, who have not met before, get into an argument in a tavern. Smith takes a punch at Jones but misses. Jones then hits Smith on the chin with his fist. Smith falls to the floor and suffers minor injuries. According to the above passage, it would be CORRECT to state that

    A. *only* Smith was justified in using physical force
    B. *only* Jones was justified in using physical force
    C. both Smith and Jones were justified in using physical force
    D. neither Smith nor Jones was justified in using physical force

8.____

9. While walking down the street, Brady observes Miller striking Mrs. Adams on the head with his fist in an attempt to steal her purse.
   According to the above passage, it would be CORRECT to state that Brady would

    A. not be justified in using deadly physical force against Miller since Brady can safety retreat
    B. be justified in using physical force against Miller, but not deadly physical force
    C. not be justified in using physical force against Miller since Brady himself is not being attacked
    D. be justified in using deadly physical force

9.____

10. Winters is attacked from behind by Sharp, who attempts to beat up Winters with a blackjack. Winters disarms Sharp and succeeds in subduing him with a series of blows to the head. Sharp stops fighting and explains that he thought Winters was the person who had robbed his apartment a few minutes before, but now realizes his mistake. According to the above passage, it would be CORRECT to state that

    A. Winters was justified in using physical force on Sharp only to the extent necessary to defend himself
    B. Winters was not justified in using physical force on Sharp since Sharp's attack was provoked by what he believed to be Winters' behavior
    C. Sharp was justified in using physical force on Winters since he reasonably believed that Winters had unlawfully robbed him
    D. Winters was justified in using physical force on Sharp only because Sharp was acting mistakenly in attacking him

10.____

11. Roberts hears a noise in the cellar of his home and, upon investigation, discovers an intruder, Welch. Welch moves towards Roberts in a threatening manner, thrusts his hand into a bulging pocket, and withdraws what appears to be a gun. Roberts thereupon strikes Welch over the head with a golf club. He then sees that the *gun* is a toy. Welch later dies of head injuries.
    According to the above passage, it would be CORRECT to state that Roberts

11.____

A. *was justified* in using deadly physical force because he reasonably believed Welch was about to use deadly physical force
B. *was not justified* in using deadly physical force
C. *was justified* in using deadly physical force only because he did not provoke Welch's conduct
D. *was justified* in using deadly physical force only because he was not the initial aggressor

Questions 12-15.

DIRECTIONS: Questions 12 through 15 are to be answered SOLELY on the basis of the following passage.

From the beginning, the Supreme Court has supervised the fairness of trials conducted by the Federal government. But the Constitution, as originally drafted, gave the court no such general authority in state oases. The court's power to deal with state cases comes from the Fourteenth Amendment, which became part of the Constitution in 1868. The crucial provision forbids any state to "deprive any person of life, liberty or property without due process of law."

The guarantee of "due process" would seem, at the least, to require fair procedure in criminal trials. But curiously, the Supreme Court did not speak on the question for many decades. During that time, however, the due process clause was interpreted to bar "unreasonable" state economic regulations, such as minimum wage laws.

In 1915, there came the case of Leo M. Frank, a Georgian convicted of murder in a trial that he contended was dominated by mob hysteria. Historians now agree that there was such hysteria, with overtones of anti-semitism.

The Supreme Court held that it could not look past the findings of the Georgia courts that there had been no mob atmosphere at the trial. Justices Oliver Wendell Holmes and Charles Evans Hughes dissented, arguing that the constitutional guarantee would be "a barren one" if the Federal courts could not make their own inferences from the facts.

In 1923, the case of Moore v. Dempsey involved five Arkansas blacks convicted of murder and sentenced to death in a community so aroused against them that at one point they were saved from lynching only by Federal troops. Witnesses against them were said to have been beaten into testifying.

The court, though not actually setting aside the convictions, directed a lower Federal court to hold a habeas corpus hearing to find out whether the trial had been fair, or whether the whole proceeding had been "a mask — that counsel, jury, and judge were swept to the fatal end by an irresistible wave of public opinion."

12. According to the above passage, the Supreme Court's INITIAL interpretation of the Fourteenth Amendment

    A. protected state supremacy in economic matters
    B. increased the scope of Federal jurisdiction
    C. required fair procedures in criminal trials
    D. prohibited the enactment of minimum wage laws

13. According to the above passage, the Supreme Court in the Frank case   13.____
    A. denied that there had been mob hysteria at the trial
    B. decided that the guilty verdict was supported by the evidence
    C. declined to question the state court's determination of the facts
    D. found that Leo Frank had not received *due process*

14. According to the above passage, the dissenting judges in the Frank case maintained that   14.____
    A. due process was an empty promise in the circumstances of that case
    B. the Federal courts could not guarantee certain provisions of the Constitution
    C. the Federal courts should not make their own inferences from the facts in state cases
    D. the Supreme Court had rendered the Constitution *barren*

15. Of the following, the MOST appropriate title for the above passage is: 15.____
    A. THE CONDUCT OF FEDERAL TRIALS
    B. THE DEVELOPMENT OF STATES' RIGHTS: 1868-1923
    C. MOORE V. DEMPSEY: A CASE STUDY IN CRIMINAL JUSTICE
    D. DUE PROCESS - THE EVOLUTION OF A CONSTITUTIONAL CORNERSTONE

KEY (CORRECT ANSWERS)

1. B
2. D
3. C
4. A
5. C

6. A
7. B
8. B
9. B
10. A

11. A
12. D
13. C
14. A
15. D

EXAMINATION SECTION
TEST 1

DIRECTIONS: Each question or incomplete statement is followed by several suggested answers or completions. Select the one that BEST answers the question or completes the statement. *PRINT THE LETTER OF THE CORRECT ANSWER IN THE SPACE AT THE RIGHT.*

Questions 1-5.

DIRECTIONS: Questions 1 through 5 are to be answered on the basis of the following fact pattern.

    Astrid's son, Carlos, attends the local high school. Carlos and another student, Manny, have been bullying another student both on and off school premises. The high school principal has notified the New York Police Department School Safety Unit of the issue. The principal has also been in touch with Astrid and Manny's mother, Mary. Mary believes Carlos is a bad influence to her son, Manny. After obtaining Astrid's phone number, Mary called Astrid and made threats towards her and Carlos. She indicated that if Carlos did not stay away from her son, Manny, she would have them both killed. The next day after school, Carlos is jumped by a group of teenagers and his leg is broken in the brawl. Astrid sues Manny, Mary, and the school district. Mary intends to countersue.

1. Who is the complainant?   1._____
   A. Manny   B. Mary   C. Astrid   D. Carlos

2. Which of the following is NOT a possible cause of action?   2._____
   A. Harassment   B. Assault
   C. Negligence   D. Breach of Contract

3. What key information is missing from the complaint?   3._____
   A. The name of the bullied student
   B. The location where Carlos was jumped
   C. The name of the high school principal
   D. The name of the police officer at the NYPD School Safety Unit who was originally notified on the issue

4. Is Mary obligated to countersue because she or her son, Manny, may have been involved in the assault against Carlos?   4._____
   A. Yes; she must answer the suit and countersue as required
   B. Yes; she must countersue to clear her son's name
   C. No; Mary is not obligated to countersue and can simply answer to the claims as alleged
   D. No; Mary is not obligated to countersue but she is obligated to countersue on Manny's behalf

5. Assume that Carlos and Manny are minors.
   What effect, if any, would this fact have on the lawsuit that is filed?
   A. The legal guardians of Carlos and Manny will need to file, and answer, the lawsuit on their behalf.
   B. Carlos and Manny do not need to appear in court.
   C. Minors cannot sue other people.
   D. The lawsuit is unaffected by their age.

6.

| Mary Williams
1 Court Way
Smithtown, NY 10170 | Mary S. Williams
1 Court Way
Smithtown, NY 10170 | Mary S. Williams
1 Court Way
Smith Town, NY 10170 |

Which selection below accurately describes the addresses as listed above?
   A. All three addresses are the same.
   B. The first and the third address are the same.
   C. None of the addresses are the same.
   D. The second and third address are the same.

Questions 7-9.

DIRECTIONS: Questions 7 through 9 are to be answered on the basis of the following table.

Schedule – Judge Presser		
Petitioner	**Respondent**	**Status**
Williams	Smith	Dismissed with prejudice
Jones	Johnson	Continued
Adams	Doe	Dismissed with prejudice
Ash	Link	Adjourned
Lam	Garcia	Settled

7. How many cases were adjourned?
   A. 3   B. 1   C. 4   D. 5

8. In how many cases were money damages awarded by the judge?
   A. 0   B. 3   C. 4   D. 5

9. How many cases will be heard again?
   A. 2   B. 1   C. 3   D. 5

10. A warrant for the arrest of Benjamin Lang. Lang lives in Suffolk County, New York. What is recorded on the warrant?
    Lang's
    A. venue   B. domicile
    C. jurisdiction   D. subject matter jurisdiction

Questions 11-13.

DIRECTIONS: Questions 11 through 13 are to be answered on the basis of the following table.

455888912	455888812	455888912	455888812
Civil Court	Civil Court	Civil Court	Civil Court
Contract	Contract	Contract	Contract
Pam L. Williams	Pam Williams	Pam Williams	Pam L. Williams

11. Which selection below accurately describes the case captions as listed above?
    A. All of the captions are the same.
    B. Caption 1 and Caption 3 are the same.
    C. Caption 2 and Caption 4 are the same.
    D. None of the captions are the same.

12. Which digit above is dissimilar in two of the above captions?
    A. The seventh digit
    B. The fifth digit
    C. The sixth digit
    D. The eighth digit

13. The notation "contract" in each caption above describes the _____ of the case.
    A. Cause of action
    B. Remedy at issue
    C. Order of the court
    D. Disposition

14. Melinda was seen stealing money from a car on Atlantic Avenue in Brooklyn. Samuel witnessed the crime from his apartment and called the police. Officer Tang recorded the call in the police log. Samuel does not own a car and reported the crime anonymously. Later that same evening, Jeremy returned his car and found the passenger window had been broken and $500 was stolen from the glove compartment. Jeremy called the police to report the crime.
In the judge's docket, the petitioner of the case against Melinda is MOST likely
    A. Jeremy
    B. Samuel
    C. Officer Tang
    D. The petitioner is anonymous

15. Judge Oswald hears cases in the Surrogate Court.
Which of the following would NOT be in Judge Oswald's court calendar?
    A. Adoption
    B. Wills
    C. Estate and Probation
    D. Negligence

Questions 16-19.

DIRECTIONS: Questions 16 through 19 are to be answered on the basis of the following fact pattern.

Judge Laredo, Smith and Ora hear no-fault cases in the 10th Judicial District throughout the week. Judge Laredo hears cases the first Monday of each month. Judge Smith hears cases with amounts in dispute over $10,000 on Tuesday, Wednesday, and Friday. Judge Ora hears cases without amounts in dispute below $25,000 on Tuesdays only.

16. Geico and ABC Chiropractic are parties to a no-fault dispute with an amount in dispute of $8,500.
    If Judge Laredo is unavailable, what day can the case be heard?
    A. Wednesday   B. Friday   C. Monday   D. Tuesday

16._____

17. Blue Health Medical and Progressive Insurance are parties to a no-fault dispute which is scheduled to be heard February 18th. Blue Health demands Progressive reimburse the provider $5,000 for the primary surgeon fees and $12,000 in assistant surgeon fees.
    Which judge will hear the matter and on which day?
    A. Judge Smith on Friday   B. Judge Smith on Tuesday
    C. Judge Smith on Wednesday   D. Judge Ora on Tuesday

17._____

18. A no-fault dispute is being heard on Monday, June 10th.
    Which statement below must be TRUE?
    A. The amount in dispute is above $10,000.
    B. The amount in dispute is less than $25,000.
    C. The amount in dispute is less than $10,000.
    D. Judge Laredo is hearing the case.

18._____

19. What information must be obtained in order to properly schedule the court calendar?
    A. The amount in dispute for each case
    B. The parties in each case
    C. Verification the dispute is "no-fault in nature"
    D. All of the above

19._____

20. A victim impact statement is an oral or _____ statement that may be read in court.
    A. recorded   B. transcribed   C. written   D. visualized

20._____

21. The clerk in the Surrogates Court will need to have access to what information in the preparation of adoption hearings?
    A. Personal information of a child's current or prior legal guardian
    B. Emancipation petition documentation
    C. Deed or will
    D. Probate documentation

21._____

Questions 22-25.

DIRECTIONS: Questions 22 through 25 are to be answered on the basis of the following table.

Schedule – Judge Orlando			
Complainant/Plaintiff	Defendant	Case Type	Money Awarded
Williams	Smith	Civil	$5,000
Jones	Johnson	Criminal	No
Adams	Doe	Criminal	$10,000
Ash	Link	Civil	$15,000
Lam	Garcia	Civil	$25,000

22. What is the total amount of money damages from civil disputes? 22.____
    A. $45,000   B. $40,000   C. $5,000   D. 0

23. Which complainant/plaintiff was awarded less than $20,000? 23.____
    A. Williams, Adams, and Ash   B. Jones, Adams, and Ash
    C. Lam, Williams, and Jones   D. Jones, Adams, and Lam

24. How many criminal cases were heard by Judge Orlando? 24.____
    A. 4   B. 5   C. 2   D. 3

25. Which defendants are responsible for paying more than $10,000? 25.____
    A. Doe and Link   B. Link and Garcia
    C. John and Doe   D. Smith and Garcia

KEY (CORRECT ANSWERS)

1. C		11. D
2. D		12. A
3. B		13. A
4. C		14. A
5. A		15. D
6. C		16. D
7. B		17. D
8. A		18. D
9. A		19. D
10. B		20. C

21. A
22. A
23. A
24. C
25. B

TEST 2

DIRECTIONS: Each question or incomplete statement is followed by several suggested answers or completions. Select the one that BEST answers the question or completes the statement. *PRINT THE LETTER OF THE CORRECT ANSWER IN THE SPACE AT THE RIGHT.*

Questions 1-4.

DIRECTIONS: Questions 1 through 4 are to be answered on the basis of the following text.

After a lengthy trial with multiple ___1___, Jim was acquitted of armed robbery and conspiracy. On the other hand, his alleged partner, Bob, was ___2___ of armed robbery. The conspiracy charge was dropped against Bob since the 12-person ___3___ found he acted alone. Jim's attorney ___4___.

1. Fill in the blank for #1:
   A. witnesses   B. evidence   C. discretionary   D. turbulent

2. Fill in the blank for #2:
   A. guilty   B. convicted   C. indicted   D. surmised

3. Fill in the blank for #3:
   A. judge   B. spectator   C. jury   D. bailiff

4. Fill in the blank for #4:
   A. appealed   B. remanded   C. reversed   D. rescinded

Questions 5-10.

DIRECTIONS: Questions 5 through 10 are to be answered on the basis of the following table.

| Court Schedule - Tuesday ||||
Judge	Total Cases	Cases Dismissed	Cases with Money Awarded
Presser	10	2	X
O'Dell	5	5	
Williams	6	6	
Sasha	8	7	X

5. How many cases were awarded money damages from Judge Presser's calendar?
   A. 2   B. 8   C. 6   D. 10

6. How many cases were awarded money damages from Judge Sasha's calendar?
   A. 8   B. 7   C. 1   D. 0

7. How many cases were dismissed on Tuesday? 7.____
   A. 11 B. 20 C. 7 D. 10

8. How many cases were awarded money damages on Tuesday? 8.____
   A. 9 B. 8 C. 1 D. 10

9. Which judge heard the MOST cases on Tuesday? 9.____
   A. Presser B. O'Dell C. Williams D. Sasha

10. Which judge heard the LEAST cases on Tuesday? 10.____
    A. Presser B. O'Dell C. Willliams D. Sasha

Questions 11-15.

DIRECTIONS: Questions 11 through 15 are to be answered on the basis of the following text.

Judge Smith hears adoption cases on Fridays. Judge Clark hears criminal cases every weekday except Tuesday in the New York City Criminal Court. Judge Clark hears felony criminal cases on Tuesday in Supreme Court. Judge Amy hears felony criminal cases on Thursday in Supreme Court.

11. Daniel is being charged with the murder of his cousin, Jerrell. 11.____
    Which judge can hear the case and on what day?
    A. Judge Smith on Friday   B. Judge Clark on Monday
    C. Judge Amy on Tuesday   D. Judge Clark on Tuesday

12. Jamal lives in Staten Island with his sister, Tisha, and Tisha's boyfriend, 12.____
    Hunter. Hunter and Jamal do not get along and one day last January, Hunter
    and Jamal were involved in a physical altercation. Hunter and Jamal both
    allege that the other assault and battered the other.
    Which judge can hear the case and on what day?
    A. Judge Clark on Tuesday   B. Judge Amy on Thursday
    C. Judge Smith on Friday   D. Judge Clark on Monday

13. Assuming the crime of assault and battery are not felonies, in which court 13.____
    will Jamal and Hunter's dispute be heard?
    A. Supreme Court   B. Surrogates Court
    C. New York City Criminal Court D. Small Claims Court

14. Assume that Tisha and Hunter have a six-year-old daughter. 14.____
    If Hunter is incarcerated for his role in the physical altercation with Jamal,
    which court would have jurisdiction over Hunter's trial?
    A. Surrogates Court   B. New York City Criminal Court
    C. Bronx Housing Court   D. Richmond County Civil Court

15. What day of the week are the MOST cases heard between all three judges? 15.____
    A. Monday B. Thursday C. Tuesday D. Friday

Questions 16-19.

DIRECTIONS: Questions 16 through 19 are to be answered on the basis of the following table.

Caption #1	Caption #2	Caption #3	Caption #4
Case 12-908	Case 12-909	Case 12-910	Case 12-911
Bronx Housing Court	Civil Court	Civil Court	Surrogates Court
Landlord/Tenant	Assault	Breach of Contract	Guardianship
ABC Property Mgmt v. Sam Smith	Jim Jones v. Sam Hunt	Terrell Williams v. Daniel Tang	In re: Jane Doe

16. Which caption above contains an INCORRECT cause of action?
    A. 1 B. 2 C. 3 D. 4

17. When were the cases in each of the captions above initiated?
    A. 2015
    B. 2016
    C. 2012
    D. Unable to determine based on the information provided

18. Which case caption above corresponds to a matter that will NOT have monetary damages awarded?
    A. 1 B. 2 C. 3 D. 4

19. Which case caption has a matter involving an institutional, rather than an individual, petitioner?
    A. 1 B. 2 C. 3 D. 4

20. A pro se litigant wants to initiate a lawsuit against his intrusive neighbor. Assuming the pro se litigant prevails, which form should be served against the neighbor after the judgment is entered?
    A. Notice of entry
    B. Notice of appeal
    C. Remand service
    D. Process discovery

21. A(n) _____ is a hearing for the purpose of determining the amount of damages sue on a claim. The clerk can enter the request on the judge's calendar after the opposing party has defaulted.
    A. imposition B. inquest C. tardy notice D. reversal

22. After a judgment is entered, it becomes enforceable for a period of time. For real property, a transcript of _____ is filed with the County Clerk which makes the judgment enforceable for a period of ten years.
    A. enforcement
    B. judgment
    C. engagement
    D. affidavit

23. Sensitive information must be _____ before it becomes public record.
    A. retained B. reposed C. redacted D. recanted

24. Service of process can be filed upon the individual or upon the _____. The affidavit of service will state the party that received the service.
    A. secretary of state
    B. guardian
    C. ad litem
    D. second most suitable person

24.____

25. A warrant can be issued to a sheriff or a marshal. The warrant clerk is responsible for reviewing the paperwork and ensuring that all is in order, including
    A. the names of the parties
    B. address of the premises
    C. the index number
    D. all of the above

25.____

KEY (CORRECT ANSWERS)

1.	A	11.	D
2.	B	12.	D
3.	C	13.	C
4.	A	14.	B
5.	B	15.	D
6.	C	16.	B
7.	B	17.	C
8.	A	18.	D
9.	A	19.	A
10.	B	20.	A

21. B
22. B
23. C
24. A
25. D

TEST 3

DIRECTIONS: Each question or incomplete statement is followed by several suggested answers or completions. Select the one that BEST answers the question or completes the statement. *PRINT THE LETTER OF THE CORRECT ANSWER IN THE SPACE AT THE RIGHT.*

1. Supreme Court clerks need to be on notice when a(n) _____ is filed as a judge is not assigned until one that parties files this document and pays the filing fee. A case will never go to trial if this document is never filed.
    A. request for maintenance
    B. request for judicial intervention
    C. remediation
    D. arbitration

1.____

Questions 2-4.

DIRECTIONS: Questions 1 through 5 are to be answered on the basis of the following chart.

Row	Case Type	Court
1	Divorce	Supreme Court
2	Custody/Visitation	Family Court
3	Child Support	Family Court
4	Paternity	Family Court
5	When Someone Dies	Surrogates Court
6	Guardianship	Surrogate's Court
7	Name Change	Supreme Court
8	Housing	New York City Housing Court

2. Assume that you are advising a pro se litigant on the proper forms to file when representing him or herself. Where would John file a small estate affidavit?
    A. Family Court
    B. Supreme Court
    C. Surrogates Court
    D. New York Civil Court

2.____

3. Where would Tom's sister, Emmanuela, file a name change?
    A. Supreme Court
    B. Family Court
    C. Surrogates Court
    D. New York City Civil Court

3.____

4. Tara and her husband, Cassidy, share custody of their twin sons, Drake and Austin. Cassidy would like to petition the court for sole custody. Where would Cassidy file his petition?
    A. New York City Housing Court
    B. Supreme Court
    C. Family Court
    D. Surrogates Court

4.____

5. Richard is representing himself in a lawsuit against his landlord. Richard does not have the financial means to hire an attorney and would like to request a reduction in the court filing fees. Richard must file a request for a _____ which is made by filing a _____ and sworn _____ which explains his finances to the court.
   A. fee waiver; notice of motion; affirmation
   B. fee waiver, notice of motion, affidavit
   C. affidavit, notice of motion, fee waiver
   D. affidavit, fee waiver, notice of motion

Questions 6-10.

DIRECTIONS: Questions 6 through 10 are to be answered on the basis of the following text.

Daniel walks into this local supermarket after lunch and falls in one of the store aisles. Daniel lies on the floor – which is nearly empty – until one of the store managers finds him, helps him up, and offers to pay for his groceries. Daniel leaves the store bruised, but not seriously injured. Two days later, Daniel falls at another grocery store. This time, Daniel threatens to sue the grocery store. The second grocery store has heard about Daniel and is concerned that he is falsifying his injuries to gain sympathy and money. The second grocery store sues Daniel to get ahead of Daniel suing them.

6. Who is the plaintiff in the case?
   A. The first grocery store
   B. The second grocery store
   C. The grocery store manager
   D. Daniel

7. Which of the following is the MOST likely cause of action in a suit that Daniel initiates against the grocery store?
   A. Breach of contract
   B. Discrimination
   C. Negligence
   D. Assault

8. After the lawsuit has commenced, which party would respond or file an answer to the complaint?
   A. Daniel
   B. The first grocery store
   C. The second grocery store
   D. The grocery store manager

9. Which party is eligible to countersue?
   A. The first grocery store
   B. The second grocery store
   C. The grocery store manager
   D. Daniel

10. The lawsuit will likely be dismissed. Why?
    A. Daniel is clearly not exaggerating his injuries.
    B. Daniel has not sued either grocery store.
    C. The store manager did not take a report of Daniel's injuries.
    D. The first grocery store must sue Daniel first.

11. A settlement between parties is not a final and binding legal agreement until the _____ of settlement is signed by both parties.
    A. amendment   B. agreement   C. stipulation   D. simulation

12. Which of the following are appropriate reasons for filing an Order to Show Cause? 12.____
    A. Changing the terms of a court order
    B. Requesting the court to dismiss a case
    C. Bringing the case back to court for any reason
    D. All of the above

13. Which of the following is NOT an appropriate reason for filing an Order to Show Case? 13.____
    A. Asking for more time to do something previously agreed upon by court order
    B. Explaining why either party missed a court date
    C. Submitting financial information for a landlord/tenant dispute
    D. Fixing errors in a stipulation

Questions 14-17.

DIRECTIONS: Questions 14 through 17 are to be answered on the basis of the following text.

Judge Chin hears child neglect and abuse cases in Family Court on Mondays and Tuesdays. Judge Amy hears divorce cases on Mondays, Wednesdays, and Fridays. Judge Snell hears child support and visitation cases every day of the week except Thursday. Termination of parental rights, foster care placement, and other child support cases are scheduled on Thursdays only with any of the three judges.

14. Tim and Sarah would like to adjust their visitation schedule for their eight-year-old daughter, Samantha. They would like the courts to assist them with this issue as they have been unable to come to an agreement on their own. Which judge will hear the case and on what day? 14.____
    A. Judge Snell on Thursday   B. Judge Snell on Monday
    C. Judge Chin on Monday   D. Judge Chin on Friday

15. Amanda would like to file for emancipation from her parents. Which judge is MOST likely to hear her case? 15.____
    A. Judge Chin
    B. Judge Amy
    C. Judge Snell'
    D. Any of the judges can hear Amanda's case

16. Jimmy and Eva are legally separating. Which judge will hear their case and on what day? 16.____
    A. Judge Chin on Monday   B. Judge Snell on Monday
    C. Judge Amy on Monday   D. Judge Chin on Tuesday

17. The State of New York intends to file a case against Eric for the abuses 17.____
and neglect of his daughter, Clare. Eric, however, is not Clare's legal guardian.
Clare's legal guardian is her grandmother, Allison. Even though it is not clear
that Clare has been neglected, the courts have found that Clare should be
placed into foster care until it can be determined who the ultimate caregiver
should be.
Which judge will MOST likely hear this case?
   A. Judge Amy
   B. Judge Chin
   C. Judge Snell
   D. Any of the judges can hear this case

Questions 18-25.

DIRECTIONS: Questions 18 through 25 are to be answered on the basis of the following chart.

Item	Fee
Obtaining an index number	$210
RJI	$95
Note of Issue	$30
Motion or Cross-Motion	$45
Demand for Jury Trial	$65
Voluntary Discontinuance	$35
Notice of Appeal	$65

18. What is the final cost to obtain an index number, demand a jury trial, and 18.____
file a notice of appeal?
   A. $210   B. $35   C. $65   D. $310

19. What is the final cost to obtain an RJI and note of issue? 19.____
   A. $125   B. $95   C. $30   D. $65

20. Which of the following is MOST likely to be filed with an RJI? 20.____
   A. Demand for jury trial   B. Notice of appeal
   C. Voluntary discontinuance   D. Obtaining an index number

21. Which of the following is the MOST likely outcome of filing a voluntary 21.____
discontinuance?
The case
   A. is automatically appealed   B. is dismissed
   C. is rescheduled   D. will be remanded

22. What is the final cost of filing a notice of appeal? 22.____
   A. $35   B. $65   C. $95   D. $120

23. What is the final cost of all items prior to filing a motion or cross-motion? 23.____
   A. $210   B. $95   C. $45   D. $335

24. Jamal would like to petition the court to compel discovery from his adversary and former friend, Bob. He would also like to speed up the date of trial by filing a demand for jury trial and RJI.
What is the final cost to do so?
A. $160   B. $95   C. $65   D. $205

25. What is the LEAST costly court document filing fee?
A. Notice of motion
B. Demand for jury trial
C. Note of issue
D. RJI

KEY (CORRECT ANSWERS)

1. B
2. C
3. A
4. C
5. B

6. B
7. C
8. A
9. D
10. B

11. C
12. D
13. C
14. B
15. D

16. C
17. D
18. D
19. A
20. D

21. B
22. B
23. D
24. D
25. C

TEST 4

DIRECTIONS: Each question or incomplete statement is followed by several suggested answers or completions. Select the one that BEST answers the question or completes the statement. *PRINT THE LETTER OF THE CORRECT ANSWER IN THE SPACE AT THE RIGHT.*

1. A lawsuit for money damages amounting to more than $25,000 can be heard in which court?
   A. Surrogates Court
   B. Supreme Court
   C. New York City Civil Court
   D. New York City Criminal Court

   1.____

2. Which of the following will NOT be on a Notice of Entry?
   A. Name of plaintiff
   B. Name of defendant
   C. Index number
   D. Social Security number

   2.____

3. Court clerks are prohibited from which of the following?
   A. Predicting the judgment of the court
   B. Explaining available options for a case or problem
   C. Providing past rulings
   D. Providing citations or copies of the law

   3.____

4. Court clerks are permitted to do all of the following EXCEPT
   A. provide forms with instructions
   B. instruct an individual on how to make a complaint
   C. analyze the law based on the specifics of a case
   D. describe court records and their availability

   4.____

5. Mary would like to sue her neighbor, Jacob, for money damages. Mary claims Jacob ran his car into Mary's garage door while it was down and caused $5,000 in damages. For claims below $1,000, the filing fee is $15, while the filing fee is $5 more for claims above $1,000.
   How much is Mary's filing fee?
   A. $15   B. $10   C. $20   D. $25

   5.____

Questions 6-10.

DIRECTIONS: Questions 6 through 10 are to be answered on the basis of the following table.

Schedule – Judge O'Neill		
Wednesday	**Thursday**	**Friday**
Continued	Dismissed with prejudice	Dismissed with prejudice
Continued	Adjourned	Continued
Settled	Dismissed with prejudice	Dismissed without prejudice
Settled	Continued	Settled
Settled	Continued	Settled

6. How many cases were adjourned this week?
   A. 5   B. 6   C. 1   D. 2

   6.____

35

7. How many cases settled this week?
   A. 5   B. 4   C. 3   D. 8

8. How many cases were dismissed this week?
   A. 6   B. 4   C. 5   D. 7

9. How many cases will likely be heard again or, in other words, how many cases can be re-filed or are otherwise continued?
   A. 6   B. 5   C. 7   D. 8

10. Which day was Judge O'Neill the LEAST busy?
    A. Thursday
    B. Friday
    C. Wednesday
    D. Each day was equally busy

Questions 11-15.

DIRECTIONS: Questions 11 through 15 are to be answered on the basis of the following text.

At Alex's arraignment, he pled ___1___ to the charge of driving under the influence and vehicular manslaughter. At trial, the prosecutor presented evidence from several ___2___ that testified Alex had a drinking problem. While Alex's defense attorneys ___3___ to that testimony and argued it was hearsay, the judge overruled those objections and allowed the testimony to be entered in the record as originally spoken. At the conclusion of the trial, Alex was found ___4___ and sentenced to community service.

11. Fill in the blank for #1:
    A. nolo   B. contendere   C. not guilty   D. guilty

12. Fill in the blank for #2:
    A. witnesses   B. evidence   C. testimony   D. bearer

13. Fill in the blank for #3:
    A. disagreed   B. objected   C. qualified   D. disclaimed

14. Fill in the blank for #4:
    A. arraigned   B. protested   C. remanded   D. guilty

15. An acquittal can also be recorded in court documentation as a finding of
    A. reversal   B. recusal   C. not guilty   D. remand

16. Evidence must be found _____ before it can be marked and evaluated by the fact finder, either a judge or jury, in civil and criminal cases.
    A. relevant   B. redacted   C. qualified   D. admissible

17. The party who seeks an appeal from a decision of a court is deemed a(n) _____ and is recorded in court documentation as such.
    A. petitioner   B. respondent   C. appellant   D. re-respondent

3 (#4)

18. How would a condominium be recorded in a bankruptcy proceeding? 18.____
    A. Real property B. Personal property
    C. Intangible asset D. chattel

19. Which of the following is LEAST likely to be recorded as a written statement 19.____
    describing one's legal and factual arguments?
    A. Attorney's brief B. Motion
    C. Summons D. Complaint

20. A lawsuit where one or more members of a large group of individuals sues 20.____
    on behalf of the other individuals in the large group is recorded as a _____
    lawsuit.
    A. introductory B. class action C. municipality D. winning

21. Jamal has filed for bankruptcy. After the trustee has reviewed Jamal's 21.____
    assets, the trustee proposes a plan to the court where Jamal promises property
    that he already owns to satisfy the major of his debt.
    The property Jamal owns that will satisfy the debt is recorded as
    A. demerits B. collateral C. debris D. probate

22. Judge Presser has rendered Emilio's sentence for the charges of armed 22.____
    robbery and kidnapping. Emilio will serve 10 years for armed robbery and 12
    years for kidnapping.
    If Emilio's total time in prison is 12 years, his sentence is recorded as
    A. consecutive B. demonstrative
    C. concurrent D. rebated

23. Assume the same facts as the previous question, but assume Emilio serves 23.____
    22 years in prison.
    In this instance, his sentence is recorded as
    A. consecutive B. demonstrative
    C. concurrent D. rebated

24. A conviction can also be recorded in court records as a judgment of 24.____
    _____ against a defendant.
    A. guilt B. remorse C. retaliation D. acquittal

25. In bankruptcy, Jamal sells his house to his mother for $5 in an effort to 25.____
    hide it from creditors who will require that he sell it to satisfy his debts.
    This sale is recorded as a
    A. fraudulent transfer B. falsified sale
    C. remarkable trade D. clawback trade

KEY (CORRECT ANSWERS)

1. B
2. D
3. A
4. C
5. C

6. C
7. A
8. B
9. A
10. C

11. C
12. A
13. B
14. D
15. C

16. D
17. C
18. A
19. C
20. B

21. B
22. C
23. A
24. A
25. A

RECORD KEEPING

EXAMINATION SECTION

TEST 1

DIRECTIONS: Each question or incomplete statement is followed by several suggested answers or completions. Select the one that BEST answers the question or completes the statement. *PRINT THE LETTER OF THE CORRECT ANSWER IN THE SPACE AT THE RIGHT.*

Questions 1-15.

DIRECTIONS: Questions 1 through 15 are to be answered on the basis of the following list of company names below. Arrange a file alphabetically, word-by-word, disregarding punctuation, conjunctions, and apostrophes. Then answer the questions.

    A Bee C Reading Materials
    ABCO Parts
    A Better Course for Test Preparation
    AAA Auto Parts Co.
    A-Z Auto Parts, Inc.
    Aabar Books
    Abbey, Joanne
    Boman-Sylvan Law Firm
    BMW Autowerks
    C Q Service Company
    Chappell-Murray, Inc.
    E&E Life Insurance
    Emcrisco
    Gigi Arts
    Gordon, Jon & Associates
    SOS Plumbing
    Schmidt, J.B. Co.

1. Which of these files should appear FIRST?   1.____
   A. ABCO Parts
   B. A Bee C Reading Materials
   C. A Better Course for Test Preparation
   D. AAA Auto Parts Co.

2. Which of these files should appear SECOND?   2.____
   A. A-Z Auto Parts, Inc.
   B. A Bee C Reading Materials
   C. A Better Course for Test Preparation
   D. AAA Auto Parts Co.

3. Which of these files should appear THIRD? 3.____
   A. ABCO Parts   B. A Bee C Reading Materials
   C. Aabar Books   D. AAA Auto Parts Co.

4. Which of these files should appear FOURTH? 4.____
   A. Aabar Books   B. ABCO Parts
   C. Abbey, Joanne   D. AAA Auto Parts Co.

5. Which of these files should appear LAST? 5.____
   A. Gordon, Jon & Associates   B. Gigi Arts
   C. Schmidt, J.B. Co.   D. SOS Plumbing

6. Which of these files should appear between A-Z Auto Parts, Inc. and Abbey, Joanne? 6.____
   A. A Bee C Reading Materials
   B. AAA Auto Parts Co.
   C. ABCO Parts
   D. A Better Course for Test Preparation

7. Which of these files should appear between ABCO Parts and Aabar Books? 7.____
   A. A Bee C Reading Materials   B. Abbey, Joanne
   C. Aabar Books   D. A-Z Auto Parts

8. Which of these files should appear between Abbey, Joanne and Boman-Sylvan Law Firm? 8.____
   A. A Better Course for Test Preparation
   B. BMW Autowerks
   C. Chappell-Murray, Inc.
   D. Aabar Books

9. Which of these files should appear between Abbey, Joanne and C Q Service? 9.____
   A. A-Z Auto Parts, Inc.   B. BMW Autowerks
   C. Choices A and B   D. Chappell-Murray, Inc.

10. Which of these files should appear between C Q Service Company and Emcrisco? 10.____
    A. Chappell-Murray, Inc.   B. E&E Life Insurance
    C. Gigi Arts   D. Choices A and B

11. Which of these files should NOT appear between C Q Service Company and E&E Life Insurance? 11.____
    A. Gordon, Jon & Associates   B. Emcrisco
    C. Gigi Arts   D. All of the above

12. Which of these files should appear between Chappell-Murray, Inc. and   12._____
    Gigi Arts?
    A. C Q Service Inc., E&E Life Insurance, and Emcrisco
    B. Emcrisco, E&E Life Insurance, and Gordon, Jon & Associates
    C. E&E Life Insurance, and Emcrisco
    D. Emcrisco and Gordon, Jon & Associates

13. Which of these files should appear between Gordon, Jon & Associates and   13._____
    SOS Plumbing?
    A. Gigi Arts   B. Schmidt, J.B. Co.
    C. Choices A and B   D. None of the above

14. Each of the choices lists the four files in their proper alphabetical order   14._____
    EXCEPT
    A. E&E Life Insurance; Gigi Arts; Gordon, Jon & Associates; SOS Plumbing
    B. E&E Life Insurance; Emcrisco; Gigi Arts; SOS Plumbing
    C. Emcrisco; Gordon, Jon & Associates; SOS Plumbing; Schmidt, J.B. Co.
    D. Emcrisco; Gigi Arts; Gordon, Jon & Associates; SOS Plumbing

15. Which of the choices lists the four files in their proper alphabetical order?   15._____
    A. Gigi Arts; Gordon, Jon & Associates; SOS Plumbing; Schmidt, J.B. Co.
    B. Gordon, Jon & Associates; Gigi Arts; Schmidt, J.B. Co.; SOS Plumbing
    C. Gordon, Jon & Associates; Gigi Arts; SOS Plumbing; Schmidt, J.B. Co.
    D. Gigi Arts; Gordon, Jon & Associates; Schmidt, J.B. Co.; SOS Plumbing

16. The alphabetical filing order of two businesses with identical names is   16._____
    determined by the
    A. length of time each business has been operating
    B. addresses of the businesses
    C. last name of the company president
    D. no one of the above

17. In an alphabetical filing system, if a business name includes a number, it should   17._____
    be
    A. disregarded
    B. considered a number and placed at the end of an alphabetical section
    C. treated as though it were written in words and alphabetized accordingly
    D. considered a number and placed at the beginning of an alphabetical
       section

18. If a business name includes a contraction (such as *don't* or *it's*), how should   18._____
    that word be treated in an alphabetical system?
    A. Divide the word into its separate parts and treat it as two words
    B. Ignore the letters that come after the apostrophe
    C. Ignore the word that contains the contraction
    D. Ignore the apostrophe and consider all letters in the contraction

19. In what order should the parts of an address be considered when using an alphabetical filing system? 19.____
    A. City or town; state; street name; house or building number
    B. State; city or town; street name; house or building number
    C. House or building number; street name; city or town; state
    D. Street name; city or town; state

20. A business record should be cross-referenced when a(n) 20.____
    A. organization is known by an abbreviated name
    B. business has a name change because of a sale, incorporation, or other reason
    C. business is known by a *coined* or common name which differs from a dictionary spelling
    D. all of the above

21. A geographical filing system is MOST effective when 21.____
    A. location is more important than name
    B. many names or titles sound alike
    C. dealing with companies who have offices all over the world
    D. filing personal and business files

Questions 22-25.

DIRECTIONS: Questions 22 through 25 are to be answered on the basis of the list of items below, which are to be filed geographically. Organize the items geographically and then answer the questions.

   I. University Press at Berkeley, U.S.
   II. Maria Sanchez, Mexico City, Mexico
   III. Great Expectations Ltd. in London, England
   IV. Justice League, Cape Town, South Africa, Africa
   V. Crown Pearls Ltd. in London, England
   VI. Joseph Prasad in London, England

22. Which of the following arrangements of the items is composed according to the policy of: *Continent, Country, City, Firm or Individual Name*? 22.____
    A. V, III, IV, VI, II, I   B. IV, V, III, VI, II, I
    C. I, IV, V, III, VI, II   D. IV, V, III, VI, I, II

23. Which of the following files is arranged according to the policy of: *Continent, Country, City, Firm or Individual Name*? 23.____
    A. South Africa; Africa; Cape Town; Justice League
    B. Mexico; Mexico City; Maria Sanchez
    C. North America; United States; Berkeley; University Press
    D. England; Europe; London; Prasad, Joseph

24. Which of the following arrangements of the items is composed according to the 24.____
    policy of: *Country, City, Firm or Individual Name*?
    A. V, VI, III, II, IV, I
    B. I, V, VI, III, II, IV
    C. VI, V, III, II, IV, I
    D. V, III, VI, II, IV, I

25. Which of the following files is arranged according to a policy of: *Country,* 25.____
    City, Firm or Individual Name?
    A. England; London; Crown Pearls Ltd.
    B. North America; United States; Berkeley; University Press
    C. Africa; Cape Town; Justice League
    D. Mexico City; Mexico; Maria Sanchez

26. Under which of the following circumstances would a phonetic filing system be 26.____
    MOST effective?
    A. When the person in charge of filing can't spell very well
    B. With large files with names that sound alike
    C. With large files with names that are spelled alike
    D. All of the above

Questions 27-29.

DIRECTIONS: Questions 27 through 29 are to be answered on the basis of the following list of numerical files.

    I.   391-023-100
    II. 361-132-170
    III. 385-732-200
    IV. 381-432-150
    V.   391-632-387
    VI. 361-423-303
    VII. 391-123-271

27. Which of the following arrangements of the files follows a consecutive-digit 27.____
    system?
    A. II, III, IV, I   B. I, V, VII, III   C. II, IV, III, I   D. III, I, V, VII

28. Which of the following arrangements follows a terminal-digit system? 28.____
    A. I, VII, II, IV, III
    B. II, I, IV, V, VII
    C. VII, VI, V, IV, III
    D. I, IV, II, III, VII

29. Which of the following lists follows a middle-digit system? 29.____
    A. I, VII, II, VI, IV, V, III
    B. I, II, VII, IV, VI, V, III
    C. VII, II, I, III, V, VI, IV
    D. VII, I, II, IV, VI, V, III

Questions 30-31.

DIRECTIONS: Questions 30 and 31 are to be answered on the basis of the following information.

   I.   Reconfirm Laura Bates appointment with James Caldecort on December 12 at 9:30 A.M.
   II. Laurence Kinder contact Julia Lucas on August 3 and set up a meeting for week of September 23 at 4 P.M.
   III. John Lutz contact Larry Waverly on August 3 and set up appointment for September 23 at 9:30 A.M.
   IV. Call for tickets for Gerry Stanton August 21 for New Jersey on September 23, flight 143 at 4:43 P.M.

30. A chronological file for the above information would be 30.____
    A. IV, III, II, I   B. III, II, IV, I   C. IV, II, III, I   D. III, I, II, IV

31. Using the above information, a chronological file for the date September 23 would be 31.____
    A. II, III, IV   B. III, I, IV   C. III, II, IV   D. IV, III, II

Questions 32-34.

DIRECTIONS: Questions 32 through 34 are to be answered on the basis of the following information.

   I.   Call Roger Epstein, Ashoke Naipaul, Jon Anderson, and Sara Washingon on April 19 at 1:00 P.M. to set up meeting with Alika D'Ornay for June 6 in New York.
   II. Call Martin Ames before noon on April 19 to confirm afternoon meeting with Bob Greenwood on April 20th.
   III. Set up meeting room at noon for 2:30 P.M. meeting on April 19th.
   IV. Ashley Stanton contact Bob Greenwood at 9:00 A.M. on April 20 and set up meeting for June 6 at 8:30 A.M.
   V.   Carol Guiland contact Shelby Van Ness during afternoon of April 20 and set up meeting for June 6 at 10:00 A.M.
   VI. Call airline and reserve tickets on June 6 for Roger Epstein trip to Denver on July 8.
   VII. Meeting at 2:30 P.M. on April 19th.

32. A chronological file for all of the above information would be 32.____
    A. II, I, III, VII, V, IV, VI   B. III, VII, II, I, IV, V, VI
    C. III, VII, I, II, V, IV, VI   D. II, III, I, VII, IV, V, VI

33. A chronological file for the date of April 19th would be 33.____
    A. II, III, VII, I   B. II, III, I, VII   C. VII, I, III, II   D. III, VII, I, II

34. Add the following information to the file, and then create a chronological file for April 20th: VIII. April 20: 3:00 P.M. meeting between Bob Greenwood and Martin Ames.
    A. IV, V, VIII B. IV, VIII, V C. VIII, V, IV D. V, IV, VIII

35. The PRIMARY advantage of computer records over a manual system is
    A. speed of retrieval
    B. accuracy
    C. cost
    D. potential file loss

KEY (CORRECT ANSWERS)

1. B	11. D	21. A	31. C
2. C	12. C	22. B	32. D
3. D	13. B	23. C	33. B
4. A	14. C	24. D	34. A
5. D	15. D	25. A	35. A
6. C	16. B	26. B	
7. B	17. C	27. C	
8. B	18. D	28. D	
9. C	19. A	29. A	
10. D	20. D	30. B	

INTERVIEWING EXAMINATION SECTION
TEST 1

DIRECTIONS: Each question or incomplete statement is followed by several suggested answers or completions. Select the one that BEST answers the question or completes the statement. *PRINT THE LETTER OF THE CORRECT ANSWER IN THE SPACE AT THE RIGHT.*

1. Of the following, the BEST way for an interviewer to calm a person who seems to have become emotionally upset as a result of a question asked is for the interviewer to

    A. talk to the person about other things for a short time
    B. ask that the person control himself
    C. probe for the cause of his emotional upset
    D. finish the questioning as quickly as possible

    1.____

2. You find that an applicant is hesitant about showing you some required personal material and documents. Your *initial* reaction to this situation should be to

    A. quietly insist that he give you the required materials
    B. make an exception in his case to avoid making him uncomfortable
    C. suspect that he may be trying to withhold evidence
    D. understand that he is in a stressful situation and may feel ashamed to reveal such information

    2.____

3. An applicant has just given you a response which does not seem clear.
Of the following, the BEST course of action for you to take in order to check your understanding of the applicant's response is for you to

    A. ask the question again during a subsequent interview with this applicant
    B. repeat the applicant's answer in the applicant's own words and ask if that is what the applicant meant
    C. later in the interview, repeat the question that led to this response
    D. repeat the question that led to this response, but say it more forcefully

    3.____

4. While speaking with applicants, you may find that there are times when an applicant will be silent for a short while before answering questions.
In order to gather the best information from the applicant, the interviewer should *generally* treat these silences by

    A. repeating the same question to make the applicant stop hesitating
    B. rephrasing the question in a way that the applicant can answer it faster
    C. directing an easier question to the applicant so that he can gain confidence in answering
    D. waiting patiently and not pressuring the applicant into quick, undeveloped answers

    4.____

5. In dealing with members of *different* ethnic and religious groups among the applicants you interview, you should give

    A. individuals the services to which they are entitled
    B. less service to those you judge to be more advantaged

    5.____

47

C. better service to groups with which you sympathize most
D. better service to groups with political "muscle"

6. You must be sure that, when interviewing an applicant, you phrase each question carefully.
Of the following, the MOST important reason for this is to insure that

   A. the applicant will phrase each of his responses carefully
   B. you use correct grammar
   C. it is clear to the applicant what information you are seeking
   D. you do not word the same question differently for different applicants

7. When given a form to complete, a client hesitates, tells you that he cannot fill out forms too well and that he is afraid he will do a poor job. He asks you to do it for him. You are quite sure, however, that he is able to do it himself.
In this case, it would be MOST advisable for you to

   A. encourage him to try filling out the application as well as he can
   B. fill out the application for him
   C. explain to him that he must learn to accept responsibility
   D. tell him that, if others can fill out an application, he can too

8. Assume that an applicant whom you are interviewing has made a statement that is obviously not true.
Of the following, the BEST course of action for you to take at this point in the interview is to

   A. ask the applicant if he is sure about his statement
   B. tell the applicant that his statement is incorrect
   C. question the applicant further to clarify his response
   D. assume that the statement is correct

9. Assume that you are conducting an *initial* interview with an applicant.
Of the following, the MOST advisable questions for you to ask at the beginning of this interview are those that

   A. can be answered in one or two sentences
   B. have nothing to do with the subject matter of the interview
   C. are most likely to reveal any hostility on the part of the applicant
   D. the applicant is most likely to be willing and able to answer

10. When interviewing a particularly nervous and upset applicant, the one of the following actions which you should take FIRST is to

    A. inform the applicant that, to be helped, he must cooperate
    B. advise the applicant that proof must be provided for statements he makes
    C. assure the applicant that every effort will be made to provide him with whatever assistance he is entitled to
    D. tell the applicant he will have no trouble so long as he is truthful

11. Assume that it is part of your job to prepare a monthly report for your unit head that eventually goes to the director. The report contains information on the number of applicants you have interviewed that have been approved and the number of applicants you have interviewed that have been turned down. Errors on such reports are *serious* because

    A. you are expected to be able to prove how many applicants you have interviewed each month
    B. accurate statistics are needed for effective management of the department
    C. they may not be discovered before the report is transmitted to the director
    D. they may result in a loss to the applicants left out of the report

12. During interviews, people give information about themselves in several ways. Which of the following *usually* gives the LEAST amount of information about the person being questioned? His

    A. spoken words
    B. tone of voice
    C. facial expression
    D. body position

13. Suppose an applicant, while being interviewed, becomes angered by your questioning and begins to use sharp, uncontrolled language.
    Which of the following is the BEST way for you to react to him?

    A. Speak in his style to show him that you are neither impressed nor upset by his speech
    B. Interrupt him and tell him that you are not required to listen to this kind of speech
    C. Lower your voice and slow the rate of your speech in an attempt to set an example that will calm him
    D. Let him continue in his way but insist that he answer your questions directly

14. You have been informed that no determination has yet been made on the eligibility of an applicant whom you have interviewed. The decision depends on further checking. His situation, however, is similar to that of many other applicants whose eligibility has been approved. The applicant, *quite worried,* calls you, and asks whether his application has been accepted.
    What would be BEST for you to do under these circumstances? Tell him

    A. his application is being checked and you will let him know the final result as soon as possible
    B. that a written request addressed to your supervisor will probably get faster action for his case
    C. not to worry since other applicants with similar backgrounds have already been accepted
    D. since there is no definite information and you are very busy, you will call him back

15. Suppose that you have been talking with an applicant. You have the feeling from the latest things the applicant has said that some of his answers to earlier questions were not totally correct. You guess that he might have been afraid or confused earlier but that your conversation has now put him in a more comfortable frame of mind.
    In order to test the reliability of information received from the earlier questions, the BEST thing for you to do *now* is to ask new questions that

A. allow the applicant to explain why he deliberately gave false information to you
B. ask for the same information, although worded differently from the original questions
C. put pressure on the applicant so that he personally wants to clear up the facts in his earlier answers
D. indicate to the applicant that you are aware of his deceptiveness

16. While providing you with required information, an applicant whom you are interviewing, informs you that she does not know certain facts.
Of the following, the MOST advisable action for you to take is to

   A. ask her to explain further
   B. advise her about research facilities
   C. express your sympathy for the situation
   D. go on to the next item of information

17. If, in an interview, you wish to determine a client's usual occupation, which one of the following questions is MOST likely to elicit the *most* useful information?

   A. Did you ever work in a factory?
   B. Do you know how to do office work?
   C. What kind of work do you do?
   D. Where are you working now?

18. Assume that you are approached by a clerk from another office who starts questioning you about one of the clients you have just interviewed. The clerk says that she is a relative of the client. According to departmental policy, all matters discussed with clients are to be kept confidential.
Of the following, the BEST course of action for you to take in this situation would be to

   A. check to see whether the clerk is really a relative before you make any further decisions
   B. explain to the clerk why you cannot divulge the information
   C. tell the clerk that you do not know the answers to her questions
   D. tell the clerk that she can get from the client any information the client wishes to give

19. Which of the following is usually the BEST technique for you, as an interviewer, to use to bring an applicant back to subject matter from which the applicant has strayed?

   A. Ask the applicant a question that is related to the subject of the interview
   B. Show the applicant that his response is unrelated to the question
   C. Discreetly reind the applicant that there is a time allotment for the interview
   D. Tell the applicant that you will be happy to discuss the extraneous matters at a future interview

20. Assume that you are interviewing a witness who is telling a story crucial to your investigation. It is important that you get all the facts being related by this witness. In order to secure this vital information, the BEST of the following techniques is to

   A. quietly interrupt the witness's story and request him to speak with deliberation so that you can record his statement
   B. guide the witness during his recital so that all important points are validated

C. confine your activities during the story to brief note-taking, and, after the information has been secured, request a full written statement
D. inform the witness that he must relate all the facts as truthfully and concisely as possible

21. The statement of any witness obtained in an interview should GENERALLY be considered

   A. as a lead requiring substantiation by additional evidence
   B. accurate if the witness appears honest and is cooperative
   C. unreliable if the witness has been involved in similar investigations
   D. as a fact admissible under the rules of evidence

22. During an important interview, an interviewer takes notes from time to time but very rarely looks at the subject being questioned.
Such action on the part of the interviewer is

   A. *unacceptable,* chiefly because during the actual interview an interviewer should pay more attention to the witness's manner of giving the information rather than to the content of his statements
   B. *acceptable,* chiefly because data should be recorded at the earliest opportunity and important data should be noted meticulously
   C. *unacceptable,* chiefly because it inhibits the person being interviewed and is not conducive to a give-and-take discussion
   D. *unacceptable,* chiefly because focusing attention on note-taking and not on the person being interviewed creates an impression of professional objectivity

23. Since he must interview persons with various personalities and attitudes, an interviewer should, *generally,* adopt a method of interviewing that

   A. is uniformly applicable to all types so that discrepancies in the accounts of individuals may be readily detected
   B. can be adjusted to the persons whom he interviews
   C. is based on the premise that most interviewees tend to be uncooperative
   D. requires the interviewer to spend as little time as possible in questioning applicants

24. One of the more difficult tasks facing an interviewer is to control the tendency of witnesses to ramble when giving information.
Of the following, the BEST technique for keeping a witness's comments pertinent is to

   A. ask questions which indicate the desired answer
   B. insist on "yes" and "no" answers to his questions
   C. construct questions that restrict the range of information which the witness can give in response
   D. ask precise questions so that the answers of the witness will necessarily be brief

25. During interviews, a certain interviewer phrases follow-up questions mentally during pauses while the subject is still answering the previous question. This practice is, *generally,*

    A. *desirable,* chiefly because it gives the impression that the interviewer is well acquainted with all the facts
    B. *undesirable,* chiefly because the interviewer cannot know whether such questions will be appropriate
    C. *desirable,* chiefly because it enables the interviewer to pose new questions without significant breaks in the discussion
    D. *undesirable,* chiefly because it subjects the person being interviewed to a barrage of questions

25.____

KEY (CORRECT ANSWERS)

1.	A	11.	B
2.	D	12.	D
3.	B	13.	C
4.	D	14.	A
5.	A	15.	B
6.	C	16.	D
7.	A	17.	C
8.	C	18.	B
9.	D	19.	A
10.	C	20.	C

21.	A
22.	C
23.	B
24.	C
25.	C

TEST 2

DIRECTIONS: Each question or incomplete statement is followed by several suggested answers or completions. Select the one that BEST answers the question or completes the statement. *PRINT THE LETTER OF THE CORRECT ANSWER IN THE SPACE AT THE RIGHT.*

1. The one of the following which is the BEST description of a *properly* objective interviewer is one who

    A. is friendly and sensitive to the client's feelings, without becoming emotionally involved
    B. is distant and impersonal, remaining unaffected by what the client says
    C. lets personal emotions enter as far as the client's situation calls for them
    D. becomes emotionally involved with the client's situation, but without showing this involvement

    1._____

2. The one of the following which is MOST necessary for successfully intefviewing a person who belongs to a culture different from that of the interviewer is for the interviewer to

    A. have some appreciation of the other culture
    B. ignore those cultural differences which lead to bias
    C. stay away from sensitive, "touchy" issues
    D. assume the mannerisms of people in the other culture

    2._____

3. In fact-finding interviews, it is generally assumed that the smaller the lumber of interviewees, the greater the increase of reliability with the addition of others.
The PROPER number of interviewees needed to insure the accuracy of information obtained *generally* depends upon the

    A. educational level of those interviewed
    B. number of people who have the required information
    C. directness of the questions asked
    D. variability of the information received

    3._____

4. The one of the following which is generally MOST likely to be *accurately* described in an interview by an interviewee is

    A. the presence of a large painting in the interviewer's office
    B. the number of people in the interviewer's waiting room
    C. space relations
    D. duration of time

    4._____

5. The one of the following which is *generally* the BEST course of action for an interviewer to take when interviewing a person who is reluctant to tell what he knows about a matter under investigation is to

    A. be curt and abrupt, and threaten the person with the consequences of his withholding information
    B. be firm and severe, and pressure the person into telling the needed information

    5._____

C. be patient and candid with the person being questioned about the investigation since doing otherwise is not ethical
D. give the person false information about the investigation so he will give the needed information without realizing its importance

6. It is often recommended that an interviewer prepare in advance a list of questions or topics to be covered in an interview.
The MAIN reason for using such a checklist is to

   A. allow investigations to be assigned to less efficient interviewers
   B. eliminate a large amount of follow-up paper work
   C. aid the interviewer in remembering to cover all important topics
   D. aid the interviewer in maintaining an objective distance from the person interviewed

7. *Usually,* the CHIEF advantage of a directive approach in an interview is that the

   A. interviewer maintains control over the course of the interview
   B. person interviewed is more likely to be put at ease
   C. person interviewed is generally left free to direct the interview
   D. interviewer will not suggest answers to the person interviewed

8. *Usually,* the CHIEF advantage of a non-directive approach in conducting an interview is that the

   A. interviewer generally conceals what he is looking for in the interview
   B. person interviewed is more likely to express his true feelings about the topic under discussion
   C. person interviewed is more likely to follow an idea introduced by the interviewer
   D. interviewer can keep the discussion limited to topics he believes to be relevant

9. The one of the following which is generally the LEAST likely to be *accurate* in a description of an event given to an interviewer is a statement about

   A. the presence of an object
   B. the number of people, when their number is small
   C. locations of people
   D. duration of time

10. Assume that you, an interviewer, are conducting a character investigation.
In an interview, the one of the following character traits of the person being interviewed which can *usually* be determined with a GOOD degree of reliability is

    A. honesty   B. dependability
    C. forcefulness   D. perseverance

11. You have been assigned the task of obtaining a family's social history.
The BEST place for you to interview members of the family while obtaining this social history would, *generally,* be in

    A. the family's home
    B. your agency's general offices
    C. the home of a friend of the family
    D. your own private office

12. If an interviewer obtains testimony from persons in interviews by means of interrogation or asking questions rather than by letting the person freely relate the testimony, what is said will, *generally,* be

    A. *greater* in range and *less* accurate
    B. *greater* in range and *more* accurate
    C. about the *same* in range and *less* accurate
    D. about the *same* in range and *more* accurate

13. Experienced interviewers have learned to phrase their questions carefully in order to obtain the desired response. Of the following, the question which would *usually* elicit the MOST accurate answer is:

    A. "How old are you?"
    B. "What is your income?"
    C. "How are you today?"
    D. "What is your date of birth?"

14. The one of the following questions which would *generally* lead to the LEAST reliable answer is:

    A. "Did you see a wallet?"
    B. "Was the German Shepherd gray?"
    C. "Didn't you see the stop sign?"
    D. "Did you see the guard on duty?"

15. Some interviewers may make a practice of observing details of the surroundings when interviewing in someone's home or office.
    Such a practice is, *generally,* considered

    A. *undesirable,* mainly because such snooping is an unwarranted, unethical invasion of privacy
    B. *undesirable,* mainly because useful information is rarely, if ever, gained this way
    C. *desirable,* mainly because useful insights into the character of the person interviewed may be gained
    D. *desirable,* mainly because it is impossible to evaluate a person adequately without such observation of his environment

KEY (CORRECT ANSWERS)

1. A	6. C	11. A
2. A	7. A	12. A
3. D	8. B	13. D
4. A	9. D	14. B
5. C	10. C	15. C

READING COMPREHENSION
UNDERSTANDING AND INTERPRETING WRITTEN MATERIAL
EXAMINATION SECTION
TEST 1

DIRECTIONS: Each question or incomplete statement is followed by several suggested answers or completions. Select the one that BEST answers the question or completes the statement. *PRINT THE LETTER OF THE CORRECT ANSWER IN THE SPACE AT THE RIGHT.*

Questions 1-2.

DIRECTIONS: Questions 1 and 2 are to be answered SOLELY on the basis of the information given in the following paragraph.

It is argued by some that the locale of the trial should be given little or no consideration. Facts are facts, they say, and if presented properly to a jury panel they will be productive of the same results regardless of where the trial is held. However, experience shows great differences in the methods of handling claims by juries. In some counties, large demands in personal injury suits are viewed with suspicion by the jury. In others, the jurors are liberal in dealing with someone else's funds.

1. According to the above paragraph, it would be ADVISABLE for an examiner on a personal injury case to

    A. get information as to the kind of verdicts that are usually awarded by juries in the county of trial
    B. give little or no consideration to the locale of the trial
    C. look for incomplete and improper presentation of facts to the jury if the verdict was not justified by the facts
    D. offer a high but realistic initial settlement figure so that no temptation is left to the claimant to gamble on the jury's verdict

2. According to the above statement, the argument that the location of a trial in a personal injury suit CANNOT counteract the weight of the evidence is

    A. basically sound
    B. disproven by the differences in awards for similar claims
    C. substantiated in those cases where the facts are properly and carefully presented to the injury
    D. supported by experience which shows great differences in the methods of handling claims by juries

Questions 3-6.

DIRECTIONS: Questions 3 through 6 are to be answered SOLELY on the basis of the following excerpt from a recorded annual report of the police department. This material should be read first and then referred to in answering these questions.

LEGAL BUREAU

One of the more important functions of this bureau is to analyze and furnish the department with pertinent information concerning Federal and State statutes and local laws which affect the department, law enforcement or crime prevention. In addition, all measure introduced in the State Legislature and the City Council which may affect this department are carefully reviewed by members of the Legal Bureau and, where necessary, opinions and recommendations thereon are prepared.

Another important function of this office is the prosecution of cases in the Criminal Courts. This is accomplished by assignment of attorneys who are members of the Legal Bureau to appear in those cases which are deemed to raise issues of importance to the department or questions of law which require technical presentation to facilitate proper determination; and also in those cases where request is made for such appearances by a judge or magistrate, some other official of the city, or a member of the force.

Proposed legislation was prepared and sponsored for introduction in the State Legislature and, at this writing, one of these proposals has already been enacted into law and five others are presently on the Governor's desk awaiting executive action. The new law prohibits the sale or possession of a hypodermic syringe or needle by an unauthorized person. The bureau's proposals awaiting executive action pertain to an amendment to the Criminal Procedure Law prohibiting desk officers from taking bail in gambling cases or in cases mentioned in the Criminal Procedure Law, including confidence men and swindlers as jostlers in the Penal Law; prohibiting the sale of switchblade knives of any size to children under 16 and bills extending the licensing period of gunsmiths.

The Legal Bureau has regularly cooperated with the Corporation Counsel and the District Attorneys in respect to matters affecting this department, and has continued to advise and represent the Police Athletic League, the Police Sports Association, the Police Relief Fund, and the Police Pension Fund.

3. Members of the Legal Bureau frequently appear in Criminal Court for the purpose of

   A. defending members of the Police Force
   B. raising issues of important to the Police Department
   C. prosecuting all offenders arrested by members of the Force
   D. facilitating proper determination of questions of law requiring technical presentation

4. The Legal Bureau sponsored a bill that would

   A. extend the licenses of gunsmiths
   B. prohibit the sale of switchblade knives to children of any size
   C. place confidence men and swindlers in the same category as jostlers in the Penal Law
   D. prohibit desk officers from admitting gamblers, confidence men, and swindlers to bail

5. One of the functions of the Legal Bureau is to

   A. review and make recommendations on proposed Federal laws affecting law enforcement
   B. prepare opinions on all measures introduced in the State Legislature and the City Council
   C. furnish the Police Department with pertinent information concerning all new Federal and State laws
   D. analyze all laws affecting the work of the Police Department

6. The one of the following that is NOT a function of the Legal Bureau is

   A. law enforcement and crime prevention
   B. prosecution of all cases in Women's Court
   C. advise and represent the Police Sports Association
   D. lecturing at the Police Academy

7. It is usual in public service for recruits to serve a probationary period before they receive tenured positions. The objective of this is to observe them in actual service, to teach them the duties of their position, and to provide a means for eliminating those who prove they are not suited for this kind of work. During this period, firings may be made at the discretion of the chief.
   Which one of the following is BEST supported by the above selection?

   A. Demonstrated fitness for the job is the basis for retention of probationary employees.
   B. Trial appointments protect the appointee from unfair dismissal practices.
   C. Public service employees need experience and instruction before permanent appointment.
   D. Exams must be given to determine the ability of probationary employees.

8. As the fundamental changes sought to be brought about in the inmates of a correctional institution can be accomplished only under good leadership, it follows that the quality of the staff whose duty it is to influence and guide the inmates in the right direction is more important than the physical facilities of the institution.
   Of the following, the MOST accurate conclusion based on the preceding statement is that

   A. the development of leadership is the fundamental change brought about in inmates by good quality staff
   B. the physical facilities of an institution are not very important in bringing about fundamental changes in the inmates
   C. with proper training the entire staff of a correctional institution can be developed into good leaders
   D. without good leadership the basic changes desired in the inmates of a correctional institution cannot be brought about

Questions 9-11.

DIRECTIONS: Questions 9 through 11 are to be answered SOLELY on the basis of the following paragraph.

The law enforcement agency is one of the most important agencies in the field of juvenile delinquency prevention. This is so not because of the social work connected with this problem, however, for this is not a police matter, but because the officers are usually the first to come in contact with the delinquent. The manner of arrest and detention makes a deep impression upon him and affects his life-long attitude toward society and the law. The juvenile court is perhaps the most important agency in this work. Contrary to the general opinion, however, it is not primarily concerned with putting children into correctional schools. The main purpose of the juvenile court is to save the child and to develop his emotional make-up in order that he can grow up to be a decent and well-balanced citizen. The system of probation is the means whereby the court seeks to accomplish these goals.

9. According to this paragraph, police work is an important part of a program to prevent juvenile delinquency because

   A. social work is no longer considered important in juvenile delinquency prevention
   B. police officers are the first to have contact with the delinquent
   C. police officers jail the offender in order to be able to change his attitude toward society and the law
   D. it is the first step in placing the delinquent in jail

9.____

10. According to this paragraph, the CHIEF purpose of the juvenile court is to

    A. punish the child for his offense
    B. select a suitable correctional school for the delinquent
    C. use available means to help the delinquent become a better person
    D. provide psychiatric care for the delinquent

10.____

11. According to this paragraph, the juvenile court directs the development of delinquents under its care CHIEFLY by

    A. placing the child under probation
    B. sending the child to a correctional school
    C. keeping the delinquent in prison
    D. returning the child to his home

11.____

Questions 12-14.

DIRECTIONS: Questions 12 through 14 are to be answered on the basis of the following paragraph.

An assassination is an act that consists of a plotted, attempted or actual murder of a prominent political figure by an individual who performs this act in other than a governmental role. This definition draws a distinction between political execution and assassination. An execution may be regarded as a political killing, but it is initiated by the organs of the state, while an assassination can always be characterized as an illegal act. A prominent figure must be the target of the killing, since the killing of lesser members of the political community is included within a wider category of internal political turmoil, namely, terrorism. Assassination is also to be distinguished from homicide. The target of the aggressive act must be a political figure rather than a private person. The killing of a prime minister by a member of an insurrectionist or underground group clearly qualifies as an assassination. So does an act by a deranged individual who tries to kill not just any individual, but the individual in his political role - as President, for example.

12. Assume that a nationally prominent political figure is charged with treason by the state, tried in a court of law, found guilty, and hanged by the state. According to the above passage, it would be MOST appropriate to regard his death as a(n)

    A. assassination
    B. execution
    C. aggressive act
    D. homicide

13. According to the above passage, which of the following statements is CORRECT?

    A. The assassination of a political figure is an illegal act.
    B. A private person may be the target of an assassination attempt.
    C. The killing of an obscure member of a political community is considered an assassination event.
    D. An execution may not be regarded as a political killing.

14. Of the following, the MOST appropriate title for this passage would be

    A. ASSASSINATION - LEGAL ASPECTS
    B. POLITICAL CAUSES OF ASSASSINATION
    C. ASSASSINATION - A DEFINITION
    D. CATEGORIES OF ASSASSINATION

Questions 15-17.

DIRECTIONS: Questions 15 through 17 are to be answered SOLELY on the basis of the following paragraph.

All applicants for an original license to operate a catering establishment shall be fingerprinted. This shall include the officers, employees, and stockholders of the company and the members of a partnership. In case of a change, by addition or substitution, occurring during the existence of a license, the person added or substituted shall be fingerprinted. However, in the case of a hotel containing more than 200 rooms, only the officer or manager filing the application is required to be fingerprinted. The police commissioner may also, at his discretion, exempt the employees and stockholders of any company. The fingerprints shall be taken on one copy of Form C.E. 20 and on two copies of C.E. 21. One copy of Form C.E. 21 shall accompany the application. Fingerprints are not required with a renewal application.

15. According to the above paragraph, an employee added to the payroll of a licensed catering establishment which is not in a hotel must be fingerprinted

    A. always
    B. unless he has been previously fingerprinted for another license
    C. unless exempted by the police commissioner
    D. only if he is the manager or an officer of the company

16. According to the above paragraph, it would be MOST accurate to state that

    A. Form C.E. 20 must accompany a renewal application
    B. Form C.E. 21 must accompany all applications
    C. Form C.E. 21 must accompany an original application
    D. both Forms C.E. 20 and C.E. 21 must accompany all applications

17. A hotel of 270 rooms has applied for a license to operate a catering establishment on the premises.
According to the instructions for fingerprinting given in the above paragraph, the _____ shall be fingerprinted.

    A. officers, employees, and stockholders
    B. officers and the manager
    C. employees
    D. officer filing the application

17.____

Questions 18-24.

DIRECTIONS: Read the following two paragraphs. Then answer the questions by selecting the answer
        A - if the paragraphs indicate it is TRUE
        B - if the paragraphs indicate it is PROBABLY true
        C - if the paragraphs indicate it is PROBABLY false
        D - if the paragraphs indicate it is FALSE

    The fallacy underlying what some might call the eighteenth and nineteenth century misconceptions of the nature of scientific investigations seems to lie in a mistaken analogy. Those who said they were investigating the structure of the universe imagined themselves as the equivalent of the early explorers and map makers. The explorers of the fifteenth and sixteenth centuries had opened up new worlds with the aid of imperfect maps; in their accounts of distant lands, there had been some false and many ambiguous statements. But by the time everyone came to believe the world was round, the maps of distant continents were beginning to assume a fairly consistent pattern. By the seventeenth century, methods of measuring space and time had laid the foundations for an accurate geography.

    On this basic issue there is far from complete agreement among philosophers *of* science today. You can, each of you, choose your side and find highly distinguished advocates for the point of view you have selected. However, in view of the revolution in physics, anyone who now asserts that science is an exploration of the universe must be prepared to shoulder a heavy burden of proof. To my mind, the analogy between the map maker and the scientist is false. A scientific theory is not even the first approximation to a map; it is not a need; it is a policy -- an economical and fruitful guide to action, by scientific investigators.

18. The author thinks that 18th and 19th century science followed the same technique as the 15th century geographers.   18.____

19. The author disagrees with the philosophers who are labelled realists.   19.____

20. The author believes there is a permanent structure to the universe.   20.____

21. A scientific theory is an economical guide to exploring what cannot be known absolutely.   21.____

22. Philosophers of science accept the relativity implications of recent research in physics.   22.____

23. It is a matter of time and effort before modern scientists will be as successful as the geographers.   23.____

24. The author believes in an indeterminate universe.   24.____

25. Borough X reports that its police force makes fewer arrests per thousand persons than any of the other boroughs.
 From this statement, it is MOST probable that

   A. sufficient information has not been given to warrant any conclusion
   B. the police force of Borough X is less efficient
   C. fewer crimes are being committed in Borough X
   D. fewer crimes are being reported in Borough X

KEY (CORRECT ANSWERS)

1. A
2. B
3. D
4. C
5. D

6. A
7. A
8. D
9. B
10. C

11. A
12. B
13. A
14. C
15. C

16. C
17. D
18. D
19. B
20. D

21. A
22. D
23. D
24. B
25. A

TEST 2

DIRECTIONS: Each question or incomplete statement is followed by several suggested answers or completions. Select the one that BEST answers the question or completes the statement. *PRINT THE LETTER OF THE CORRECT ANSWER IN THE SPACE AT THE RIGHT.*

Questions 1-2.

DIRECTIONS: Questions 1 and 2 are to be answered on the basis of the information given in the following passage.

Assume that a certain agency is having a problem at one of its work locations because a sizable portion of the staff at that location is regularly tardy in reporting to work. The management of the agency is primarily concerned about eliminating the problem and is not yet too concerned about taking any disciplinary action. An investigator is assigned to investigate to determine, if possible, what might be causing this problem.

After several interviews, the investigator sees that low morale created by poor supervision at this location is at least part of the problem. In addition, there is a problem of tardiness and lack of interest.

1. Given the goals of the investigation and assuming that the investigator was using a non-directive approach in this interview, of the following, the investigator's MOST effective response should be:

    A. You know, you are building a bad record of tardiness
    B. Can you tell me more about this situation?
    C. What kind of person is your superior?
    D. Do you think you are acting fairly towards the agency by being late so often?

1.____

2. Given the goals of the investigation and assuming the investigator was using a directed approach in this interview, of the following, the investigator's response should be:

    A. That doesn't seem like much of an excuse to me
    B. What do you mean by saying that you've lost interest?
    C. What problems are there with the supervision you are getting?
    D. How do you think your tardiness looks in your personnel record?

2.____

Questions 3-5.

DIRECTIONS: Questions 3 through 5 are to be answered SOLELY on the basis of the following passage.

As investigators, we are more concerned with the utilitarian than the philosophical aspects of ethics and ethical standards, procedures, and conduct. As a working consideration, we might view ethics as the science of doing the right thing at the right time in the right manner in conformity with the normal, everyday standards imposed by society; and in conformity with the judgment society would be expected to make concerning the rightness or wrongness of what we have done.

An ethical code might be considered a basic set of rules and regulations to which we must conform in the performance of investigative duties. Ethical standards, procedures, and conduct might be considered the logical workings of our ethical code in its everyday application to our work. Ethics also necessarily involves morals and morality. We must eventually answer the self-imposed question of whether or not we have acted in the right way in conducting our investigative activities in their individual and total aspects.

3. Of the following, the MOST suitable title for the above passage is

    A. THE IMPORTANCE OF RULES FOR INVESTIGATORS
    B. THE BASIC PHILOSOPHY OF A LAWFUL SOCIETY
    C. SCIENTIFIC ASPECTS OF INVESTIGATIONS
    D. ETHICAL GUIDELINES FOR THE CONDUCT OF INVESTIGATIONS

4. According to the above passage, ethical considerations for investigators involve

    A. special standards that are different from those which apply to the rest of society
    B. practices and procedures which cannot be evaluated by others
    C. individual judgments by investigators of the appropriateness of their own actions
    D. regulations which are based primarily upon a philosophical approach

5. Of the following, the author's PRINCIPAL purpose in writing the above passage seems to have been to

    A. emphasize the importance of self-criticism in investigative activities
    B. explain the relationship that exists between ethics and investigative conduct
    C. reduce the amount of unethical conduct in the area of investigations
    D. seek recognition by his fellow investigators for his academic treatment of the subject matter

Questions 6-8.

DIRECTIONS: Questions 6 through 8 are to be answered SOLELY on the basis of the following passage.

The investigator must remember that acts of omission can be as effective as acts of commission in affecting the determination of disputed issues. Acts of omission, such as failure to obtain available information or failure to verify dubious information, manifest themselves in miscarriages of justice and erroneous adjudications. An incomplete investigation is an erroneous investigation because a conclusion predicated upon inadequate facts is based on quicksand.

When an investigator throws up his hands and admits defeat, the reason for this action does not necessarily lie in his possible laziness and ineptitude. It is more likely that the investigator has made his conclusions after exhausting only those avenues of investigation of which he is aware. He has exercised good faith in his belief that nothing else can be done.

This tendency must be overcome by all investigators if they are to operate at top efficiency. If no suggestion for new or additional action can be found in any authority, an investigator should use his own initiative to cope with a given situation. No investigator should ever hesitate to set precedents. It is far better in the final analysis to attempt difficult solutions, even if the chances of error are obviously present, than it is to take refuge in the spineless adage: If you don't do anything, you don't do it wrong.

6. Of the following, the MOST suitable title for the above passage is

    A. THE NEED FOR RESOURCEFULNESS IN INVESTIGATIONS
    B. PROCEDURES FOR COMPLETING AN INVESTIGATION
    C. THE DEVELOPMENT OF STANDARDS FOR INVESTIGATORS
    D. THE CAUSES OF INCOMPLETE INVESTIGATIONS

7. Of the following, the author of this passage considers that the LEAST important consideration in developing new investigative methods is

    A. efficiency   B. caution
    C. imagination   D. thoroughness

8. According to this passage, which of the following statements is INCORRECT?

    A. Lack of creativity may lead to erroneous investigations.
    B. Acts of omission are sometimes as harmful as acts of commission.
    C. Some investigators who give up on a case are lazy or inept.
    D. An investigator who gives up on a case is usually not acting in good faith.

Questions 9-12.

DIRECTIONS: Questions 9 through 12 are to be answered on the basis of the following paragraph.

A report of investigation should not be weighed down by a mass of information which is hardly material or only remotely relevant, or which fails to prove a point, clarify an issue, or aid the inquiry even by indirection. Some investigative agencies, however, value the report for its own sake, considering it primarily as a justification of the investigative activity contained therein. Every step is listed to show that no logical measure has been overlooked and to demonstrate that the reporting agent is beyond criticism. This system serves to provide reviewing authorities with a ready means of checking subordinates and provides order, method, and routine to investigative activity. In addition, it may offer supervisors and investigators a sense of security; the investigator would know within fairly exact limits what is expected of him and the supervisor may be comforted by the knowledge that his organization may not be reasonably criticized in a particular case on the grounds of obvious omissions or inertia. To the state's attorney and others, however, who must take administrative action on the basis of the report, the irrelevant and immaterial information thwarts the purpose of the investigation by dimming the issues and obscuring the facts that are truly contributory to the proof.

9. From the point of view of the supervising investigator, a drawback of having the investigator prepare the type of report which the state's attorney would like is that it

    A. gives a biased and one-sided view of what should have been an impartial investigation
    B. has only limited usefulness as an indication that all proper investigative methods were used by the investigator
    C. overlooks logical measures, removing the responsibility for taking those measures which the investigator should otherwise have been expected to take
    D. sets fairly exact limits to what the supervisor can expect of the investigator

10. District attorneys do not like reports of investigations in which every step is listed because

    A. their administrative action is then based on irrelevant and immaterial information
    B. it places the investigator beyond criticism, making the responsibility of the district attorney that much greater
    C. of the difficulty of finding among the mass of information the portion which is meaningful and useful
    D. the inclusion of indirect or hardly material information is not in accord with the order in which the steps were taken

11. As expressed in the above paragraph, the type of report which MOST investigators prefer to prepare is

    A. a step-by-step account of their activities, including both fruitful and unfruitful steps, since to do so provides order and method and gives them a sense of security
    B. not made clear, even though current practice in some agencies is to include every step taken in the investigation
    C. one from which useless and confusing information has been excluded because it is not helpful and is poor practice
    D. one not weighed down by a mass of irrelevant information but one which shows within fairly exact limits what was expected of them

12. With regard to the type of information which an investigator should include in his report, the above paragraph expresses the opinion that

    A. it is best to include in the report only that information which supports the conclusions of the investigator
    B. reports should include all relevant and clarifying information and exclude information on inquiries which had no productive result
    C. reports should include sufficient information to demonstrate that the investigator has been properly attending to his duties and all the information which contributes toward proof of what occurred in the case
    D. the most logical thing to do is to list every step in the investigation and its result

Questions 13-17.

DIRECTIONS: Questions 13 through 17 are to be answered SOLELY on the basis of the following paragraph.

    Those statutes of limitations which are of interest to a claim examiner are the ones affecting third party actions brought against an insured covered by a liability policy of insurance. Such statutes of limitations are legislative enactments limiting the time within which such actions at law may be brought. Research shows that such periods differ from state to state and vary within the states with the type of action brought. The laws of the jurisdiction in which the action is brought govern and determine the period within which the action may be instituted, regardless of the place of the cause of action or the residence of the parties at the time of cause of action. The period of time set by a statute of limitations for a tort action starts from the moment the alleged tort is committed. The period usually extends continuously until its expiration, upon which legal action may no longer be brought. However, there is a suspension of the running of the period when a defendant has concealed himself in order to avoid service of legal process. The suspension continues until the defendant discontinues his concealment and then the period starts running again. A defendant may, by his agreement or conduct, be legally barred from asserting the statute of limitations as a defense to an action. The insurance carrier for the defendant may, by the misrepresentation of the claims man, cause such a bar against use of the statute of limitations by the defendant. If the claim examiner of the insurance carrier has by his conduct or assertion lulled the plaintiff into a false sense of security by false representations, the defendant may be barred from setting up the statute of limitations as a defense.

13. Of the following, the MOST suitable title for the above paragraph is

    A. FRAUDULENT USE OF THE STATUTE OF LIMITATIONS
    B. PARTIES AT INTEREST IN A LAWSUIT
    C. THE CLAIM EXAMINER AND THE LAW
    D. THE STATUTE OF LIMITATIONS IN CLAIMS WORK

14. The period of time during which a third party action may be brought against an insured covered by a liability policy depends on

    A. the laws of the jurisdiction in which the action is brought
    B. where the cause of action which is the subject of the suit took place
    C. where the claimant lived at the time of the cause of action
    D. where the insured lived at the time of the cause of action

15. Time limits in third party actions which are set by the statutes of limitations described above are

    A. determined by claimant's place of residence at start of action
    B. different in a state for different actions
    C. the same from state to state for the same type of action
    D. the same within a state regardless of type of action

16. According to the above paragraph, grounds which may be legally used to prevent a defendant from using the statute of limitations as a defense in the action described are

    A. defendant's agreement or concealment; a charge of liability for death and injury
    B. defendant's agreement or conduct; misrepresentation by the claims man
    C. fraudulent concealment by claim examiner; a charge of liability for death or injury; defendant's agreement
    D. misrepresentation by claim examiner of carrier; defendant's agreement; plaintiff's concealment

17. Suppose an alleged tort was commited on January 1, 2008 and that the period in which action may be taken is set at three years by the statute of limitations. Suppose further that the defendant, in order to avoid service of legal process, had concealed himself from July 1, 2010 through December 31, 2010.
    In this case, the defendant may not use the statute of limitations as a defense unless action is brought by the plaintiff after _____, 2011.

    A. January 1   B. February 28
    C. June 30   D. August 1

Questions 18-20.

DIRECTIONS: Questions 18 through 20 are to be answered SOLELY on the basis of information contained in the following passage.

No matter how well the interrogator adjusts himself to the witness and how precisely he induces the witness to describe his observations, mistakes still can be made. The mistakes made by an experienced interrogator may be comparatively few, but as far as the witness is concerned, his path is full of pitfalls. Modern *witness psychology* has shown that even the most honest and trustworthy witnesses are apt to make grave mistakes in good faith. It is, therefore, necessary that the interrogator get an idea of the weak links in the testimony in order to check up on them in the event that something appears to be strange or not quite satisfactory.

Unfortunately, modern witness psychology does not yet offer any means of directly testing the credibility of testimony. It lacks precision and method, in spite of worthwhile attempts on the part of learned men. At the same time, witness psychology, through the gathering of many experiences concerning the weaknesses of human testimony, has been of invaluable service. It shows clearly that only evidence of a technical nature has absolute value as proof.

Testimony may be separated into the following stages: (1) perception, (2) observation, (3) mind fixation of the observed occurrences, in which fantasy, association of ideas, and personal judgment participate, and (4) expression in oral or written form, where the testimony is transferred from one witness to another or to the interrogator.

Each of these stages offers innumerable possibilities for the distortion of testimony.

18. The above passage indicates that having witnesses talk to each other before testifying is a practice which is GENERALLY

    A. *desirable,* since the witnesses will be able to correct each other's errors in observation before testimony
    B. *undesirable,* since the witnesses will collaborate on one story to tell the investigator
    C. *undesirable,* since one witness may distort his testimony because of what another witness may erroneously say
    D. *desirable,* since witnesses will become aware of discrepancies in their own testimony and can point out the discrepancies to the investigator

19. According to the above passage, the one of the following which would be the MOST reliable for use as evidence would be the testimony of a

    A. handwriting expert about a signature on a forged check
    B. trained police officer about the identity of a criminal
    C. laboratory technician about an accident he has observed
    D. psychologist who has interviewed any witnesses who relate conflicting stories

20. Concerning the validity of evidence, it is CLEAR from the above passage that

    A. only evidence of a technical nature is at all valuable
    B. the testimony of witnesses is so flawed that it is usually valueless

C. an investigator, by knowing modern witness psychology, will usually be able to perceive mistaken testimony
D. an investigator ought to expect mistakes in even the most reliable witness testimony

Questions 21-22.

DIRECTIONS: Questions 21 and 22 are to be answered SOLELY on the basis of the information contained in the passage below. This passage represents a report prepared by a subordinate superior concerning a school demonstration.

On April 1, a group of students, each holding an anti-apartheid sign, was involved in a demonstration on the grounds of Columbia University. The students began by locking the main entrance doors to the Administration Building and preventing faculty and students from entering or leaving the building.

The C.O. of the police detail at the scene requested additional assistance of four female detectives, an Emergency Service van, and a police photographer equipped with a Polaroid instamatic camera.

When the additional assistance arrived, the Commanding Officer directed the students to disperse. His justification for the order was that the demonstrators were violating the rights of other students and certain faculty members by denying them access to the Administration Building. The students ignored the order to disperse and the Commanding Officer of the police detail ordered them to be removed.

Another group of students who had been standing in front of the library were sympathetic toward the demonstrators and charged the police. Several police officers were injured during the ensuing hostilities.

Eventually, order was restored. That evening, the television coverage presented a neutral and fairly accurate account of the incident.

21. Which of the following statements MOST clearly and accurately reflects the contents of the report?   21.____

    A. A large group of students, all of whom were holding anti-apartheid signs, was involved in a demonstration on the grounds of Columbia University.
    B. A large group of students, some of whom were holding anti-apartheid signs, was involved in a demonstration on the grounds of Columbia University.
    C. Each of a group of Columbia students carrying anti-apartheid signs was involved in a demonstration on the grounds of Columbia University.
    D. Each of the students involved in the demonstration on the grounds of Columbia University was holding an anti-apartheid sign.

22. Which of the following statements MOST clearly and accurately reflects the contents of the report?   22.____

A. The Commanding Officer of the police detail justified his order that the demonstrators disperse when the additional assistance arrived.
B. When the additional assistance arrived, the Commanding Officer of the police detail justified his order that the demonstrators disperse.
C. The Commanding Officer of the police detail directed the students to disperse when the additional assistance arrived.
D. The Commanding Officer of the police detail requested additional assistance because the student demonstrators were violating the rights of other students and certain faculty members.

23. Which of the following statements MOST clearly and accurately reflects the contents of the report?

    A. Another group of students charged the police because they were sympathetic toward the police.
    B. The evening television coverage of the demonstration was fair and accurate.
    C. The group of students who had been standing in front of the library was sympathetic toward the demonstrators.
    D. Several police officers were injured during the hostilities which took place in front of the library.

Questions 24-25.

DIRECTIONS: Questions 24 and 25 are to be answered SOLELY on the basis of the information given in the following paragraph.

Credibility of a witness is usually governed by his character and is evidenced by his reputation for truthfulness. Personal or financial reasons or a criminal record may cause a witness to give false information to avoid being implicated. Age, sex, physical and mental abnormalities, loyalty, revenge, social and economic status, indulgence in alcohol, and the influence of other persons are some of the many factors which may affect the accuracy, willingness, or ability with which witnesses observe, interpret, and describe occurrences.

24. According to the above paragraph, a witness may, for personal reasons, give wrong information about an occurrence because he

    A. wants to protect his reputation for truthfulness
    B. wants to embarrass the investigator
    C. doesn't want to become involved
    D. doesn't really remember what happened

25. According to the above paragraph, factors which influence the witness of an occurrence may affect

    A. not only what he tells about it but what he was able and wanted to see of it
    B. only what he describes and interprets later but not what he actually sees at the time of the event
    C. what he sees but not what he describes
    D. what he is willing to see but not what he is able to see

KEY (CORRECT ANSWERS)

1. B
2. C
3. D
4. C
5. B

6. A
7. B
8. D
9. B
10. C

11. B
12. B
13. D
14. A
15. B

16. B
17. C
18. C
19. A
20. D

21. D
22. C
23. C
24. C
25. A

EXAMINATION SECTION
TEST 1

DIRECTIONS: Each question or incomplete statement is followed by several suggested answers or completions. Select the one that BEST answers the question or completes the statement. *PRINT THE LETTER OF THE CORRECT ANSWER IN THE SPACE AT THE RIGHT.*

Questions 1-9.

DIRECTIONS: Questions 1 through 9 consist of sentences which may or may not be examples of good English usage. Consider grammar, punctuation, spelling, capitalization, awkwardness, etc. Examine each sentence, and then choose the correct statement about it from the four choices below it. If the English usage in the sentence given is better than it would be with any of the changes suggested in options B, C, and D, choose option A. Do not choose an option that will change the meaning of the sentence.

1. According to Judge Frank, the grocer's sons found guilty of assault and sentenced last Thursday.

    A. This is an example of acceptable writing.
    B. A comma should be placed after the word *sentenced*.
    C. The word *were* should be placed after *sons*
    D. The apostrophe in *grocer's* should be placed after the *s*.

2. The department heads assistant said that the stenographers should type duplicate copies of all contracts, leases, and bills.

    A. This is an example of acceptable writing.
    B. A comma should be placed before the word *contracts*.
    C. An apostrophe should be placed before the *s* in *heads*.
    D. Quotation marks should be placed before *the stenographers* and after *bills*.

3. The lawyers questioned the men to determine who was the true property owner?

    A. This is an example of acceptable writing.
    B. The phrase *questioned the men* should be changed to *asked the men questions*.
    C. The word *was* should be changed to *were*.
    D. The question mark should be changed to a period.

4. The terms stated in the present contract are more specific than those stated in the previous contract.

    A. This is an example of acceptable writing.
    B. The word *are* should be changed to *is*.
    C. The word *than* should be changed to *then*.
    D. The word *specific* should be changed to *specified*.

5. Of the lawyers considered, the one who argued more skillful was chosen for the job.

    A. This is an example of acceptable writing.
    B. The word *more* should be replaced by the word *most*.
    C. The word *skillful* should be replaced by the word *skillfully,*
    D. The word *chosen* should be replaced by the word *selected*.

6. Each of the states has a court of appeals; some states have circuit courts.   6._____

    A. This is an example of acceptable writing.
    B. The semi-colon should be changed to a comma.
    C. The word *has* should be changed to *have*.
    D. The word *some* should be capitalized.

7. The court trial has greatly effected the child's mental condition.   7._____

    A. This is an example of acceptable writing.
    B. The word *effected* should be changed to *affected*.
    C. The word *greatly* should be placed after *effected*.
    D. The apostrophe in *child's* should be placed after the *s*.

8. Last week, the petition signed by all the officers was sent to the Better Business Bureau.   8._____

    A. This is an example of acceptable writing.
    B. The phrase *last week* should be placed after *officers*.
    C. A comma should be placed after *petition*.
    D. The word *was* should be changed to *were*.

9. Mr. Farrell claims that he requested form A-12, and three booklets describing court procedures.   9._____

    A. This is an example of acceptable writing.
    B. The word *that* should be eliminated.
    C. A colon should be placed after *requested*.
    D. The comma after *A-12* should be eliminated.

Questions 10-21.

DIRECTIONS: Questions 10 through 21 contain a word in capital letters followed by four suggested meanings of the word. For each question, choose the BEST meaning for the word in capital letters.

10. SIGNATORY - A   10._____

    A. lawyer who draws up a legal document
    B. document that must be signed by a judge
    C. person who signs a document
    D. true copy of a signature

11. RETAINER - A   11._____

    A. fee paid to a lawyer for his services
    B. document held by a third party
    C. court decision to send a prisoner back to custody pending trial
    D. legal requirement to keep certain types of files

12. BEQUEATH - To   12._____

    A. receive assistance from a charitable organization
    B. give personal property by will to another
    C. transfer real property from one person to another
    D. receive an inheritance upon the death of a relative

13. RATIFY - To

    A. approve and sanction
    B. forego
    C. produce evidence
    D. summarize

14. CODICIL - A

    A. document introduced in evidence in a civil action
    B. subsection of a law
    C. type of legal action that can be brought by a plaintiff
    D. supplement or an addition to a will

15. ALIAS

    A. Assumed name
    B. In favor of
    C. Against
    D. A writ

16. PROXY - A(n)

    A. phony document in a real estate transaction
    B. opinion by a judge of a civil court
    C. document containing appointment of an agent
    D. summons in a lawsuit

17. ALLEGED

    A. Innocent
    B. Asserted
    C. Guilty
    D. Called upon

18. EXECUTE - To

    A. complete a legal document by signing it
    B. set requirements
    C. render services to a duly elected executive of a municipality
    D. initiate legal action such as a lawsuit

19. NOTARY PUBLIC - A

    A. lawyer who is running for public office
    B. judge who hears minor cases
    C. public officer, one of whose functions is to administer oaths
    D. lawyer who gives free legal services to persons unable to pay

20. WAIVE - To

    A. disturb a calm state of affairs
    B. knowingly renounce a right or claim
    C. pardon someone for a minor fault
    D. purposely mislead a person during an investigation

21. ARRAIGN - To

    A. prevent an escape
    B. defend a prisoner
    C. verify a document
    D. accuse in a court of law

Questions 22-40.

DIRECTIONS: Questions 22 through 40 each consist of four words which may or may not be spelled correctly. If you find an error in
only one word, mark your answer A;
any two words, mark your answer B;
any three words, mark your answer C;
none of these words, mark your answer D.

22.	occurrence	Febuary	privilege	similiar	22._____
23.	separate	transferring	analyze	column	23._____
24.	develop	license	bankrupcy	abreviate	24._____
25.	subpoena	arguement	dissolution	foreclosure	25._____
26.	exaggerate	fundamental	significance	warrant	26._____
27.	citizen	endorsed	marraige	appraissal	27._____
28.	precedant	univercity	observence	preliminary	28._____
29.	stipulate	negligence	judgment	prominent	29._____
30.	judisial	whereas	release	guardian	30._____
31.	appeal	larcenny	transcrip	jurist	31._____
32.	petition	tenancy	agenda	insurance	32._____
33.	superfical	premise	morgaged	maintainance	33._____
34.	testamony	publically	installment	possessed	34._____
35.	escrow	decree	eviction	miscelaneous	35._____
36.	securitys	abeyance	adhere	corporate	36._____
37.	kaleidoscope	anesthesia	vermilion	tafetta	37._____
38.	congruant	barrenness	plebescite	vigilance	38._____
39.	picnicing	promisory	resevoir	omission	39._____
40.	supersede	banister	wholly	seize	40._____

KEY (CORRECT ANSWERS)

1.	C	11.	A	21.	D	31.	B
2.	C	12.	B	22.	B	32.	D
3.	D	13.	A	23.	D	33.	C
4.	A	14.	D	24.	B	34.	B
5.	C	15.	A	25.	A	35.	A
6.	A	16.	C	26.	D	36.	A
7.	B	17.	B	27.	B	37.	A
8.	A	18.	A	28.	C	38.	B
9.	D	19.	C	29.	D	39.	C
10.	C	20.	B	30.	A	40.	D

EXAMINATION SECTION
TEST 1

DIRECTIONS: Each question or incomplete statement is followed by several suggested answers or completions. Select the one that BEST answers the question or completes the statement. *PRINT THE LETTER OF THE CORRECT ANSWER IN THE SPACE AT THE RIGHT.*

1. An affidavit and a summons are similar in that an affidavit and a summons
   A. both require an answer
   B. both may be filed with a court of proper jurisdiction
   C. outline the particulars of the case
   D. are both served on each party in a lawsuit

2. A judgment of the court refers to a(n)
   A. final order and decision on a matter before the Court that is binding on both parties
   B. reservation by the judge to defer a decision to a later date
   C. award by the judge granting monetary payment to the plaintiff
   D. request by the defendant to dismiss the case against the plaintiff

3. A pretrial conference typically requires the presence of the
   A. attorneys representing the parties and the case and the judge
   B. judge only
   C. named parties in the lawsuit and the judge
   D. named parties in the lawsuit, attorneys, and the judge

4. Gary, a local business owner, has discovered one of his customers is suing him for monetary and punitive damages in court. Gary would like to represent himself at trial.
   Gary is a(n) _____ litigant.
   A. Qui Tam   B. In Limine   C. Pro Se   D. Pro Tem

5. A subpoena duces tecum requires its recipient to
   A. appear and produce documents   B. appear and provide testimony
   C. appear with a witness   D. appear

6. A capital offense is characterized by its punishment. A capital offense is punishable by
   A. large money payment, payable in a lump sum
   B. lien on real property
   C. death
   D. an automatic sentence of 20 years

7. Bankruptcy law is governed by _____ law, rather than _____ law. Therefore, bankruptcy hearings are heard in _____ courts.
   A. State, Federal, District
   B. District, State, Federal
   C. Federal, District, State
   D. Federal, State, District

8. Michelle is the subject of a wage garnishment. She is a full-time student at Brooklyn College and also works full time as an administrative assistant for an accountant in Queens. After receiving notice of the wage garnishment, she decides to quit her job and take a part-time job as a receptionist at a dental office.
   Are Michelle's dental office wages subject to garnishment?
   A. No, because she is only working part time.
   B. No, because the garnishment was issued while she was working at her last job.
   C. Yes, because she obtained new employment.
   D. Yes.

9. A trial which was scheduled to begin in Queens in October is now being moved to Albany. The trial is still scheduled to begin in October.
   The change of the trial location is an example of a change in
   A. venue
   B. locale
   C. environment
   D. jurisdiction

10. Plaintiff's attorney has withdrawn as counsel and is being replaced by another attorney who comes highly recommended by a family friend of the plaintiff.
    Where is the change of attorney MOST appropriately recorded?
    A. Disclosure statement
    B. Docket
    C. Letter to the Judge
    D. Deposition

11. A bench trial is a trial without a(n)
    A. plaintiff's attorney
    B. jury
    C. defendant's attorney
    D. bailiff

12. Mark's son, Jeff, has been arrested and is being held on $50,000 bail. Mark is visibly upset and angrily demands to know why bail is required in order for Jeff to be released from prison.
    The MOST correct answer is:
    A. Bail is absolutely required of all prisoners awaiting trial.
    B. Bail is required to release Jeff because he committed a felony.
    C. Bail is not always required, but can be established to ensure a person's appearance at court when required.
    D. Bail is only required when a probation officer has not yet been assigned.

13. In classifying her debts in bankruptcy, Alicia attests that she owes $10,000 in personal credit card debt, $5,000 business loan to a credit union, and $200,000 mortgage.
    Which debts will be classified as consumer debt?
    A. Credit card debt, business loan, and mortgage
    B. The business loan only
    C. Credit card debt and business loans
    D. Credit card debt and mortgage

13.____

14. A warrant has been issued by Judge Walker for John Smith. There are typically two types of warrants that can be issued.
    They are
    A. search and arrest
    B. seize and arrest
    C. detain and arrest
    D. summons and arrest

14.____

15. The role of the court stenographer is to
    A. assist the bailiff in maintaining order in the courtroom
    B. serve as an additional support to the court clerk
    C. transcribe the dialogue of court proceedings in short form to create the trial transcript
    D. record the final judgment and transcribe the judge's rationale for sentencing

15.____

16. Precedent refers to:
    A. The same plaintiff and same defendant from another lawsuit are named in the present suit
    B. A defendant is on trial again after being found innocent in an earlier trial
    C. An earlier case or decision of a court that is considered authority in the present case because of an identical or similar question of law
    D. A series of lawsuits involving the same plaintiff in each case

16.____

17. An automatic stay has what effect on a debtor in a bankruptcy petition?
    A. Allows the debtor to appoint a trustee for his/her petition
    B. Stops lawsuits, foreclosures, garnishments, and most collection activities against the debtor the moment a bankruptcy petition is filed
    C. Provides the debtor with additional time to arrange their assets before filing the petition
    D. Allows the debtor to attend court hearings on the status of their bankruptcy petition

17.____

18. A joint petition in bankruptcy refers to a bankruptcy
    A. petition filed by a husband and wife together
    B. petition filed by business partners
    C. petition filed by family members
    D. petitioned by the largest creditor of the debtor

18.____

19. A misdemeanor is punishable by _____ or _____, whereas a felony is punishable by _____ or _____.
    A. two years, less; two years, more
    B. six months, less; six months, more
    C. one year, less; one year, more
    D. one year, more; one year, less

20. Gail has filed for Chapter 7 bankruptcy. She has read online that some of her property will be considered non-exempt assets. Non-exempt assets is property that
    A. can be sold to satisfy claims of the creditors
    B. is exempt from being included in the bankruptcy estate
    C. does not need to be reported to the trustee
    D. can be considered "charge offs" for tax purposes

21. A motion represents a _____ to the court, requiring a decision by the judge.
    A. request   B. demand   C. action   D. plea

22. A jury verdict that a criminal defendant is not guilty, or a finding by a judge that there is insufficient evidence to support a conviction is known as a(n)
    A. information
    B. acquiescence
    C. acquittal
    D. compromise in settlement

23. An affidavit is accurately defined as a(n)
    A. statement made in the presence of a court of competent jurisdiction
    B. written statement that is notarized then sent to a court of competent jurisdiction
    C. oral statement transcribed by his or her attorney
    D. written or printed statement made under oath

24. Under what circumstances does an alternate juror help decide a case?
    A. Only when called on to replace a regular juror
    B. When a regular juror has trouble making a decision in the case
    C. When the bailiff asks the alternate jurors' opinion on the case
    D. Only during bench trials

25. A case that is dismissed with prejudice prevents which of the following: The filing of
    A. an identical suit in a later filing
    B. a suit by the same plaintiff in a later filing
    C. a suit by the same defendant in a later filing
    D. the same suit in the same courthouse in a later filing

KEY (CORRECT ANSWERS)

1.	B	11.	B
2.	A	12.	C
3.	A	13.	D
4.	C	14.	A
5.	A	15.	C
6.	C	16.	C
7.	D	17.	B
8.	D	18.	A
9.	A	19.	C
10.	B	20.	A

21. A
22. C
23. D
24. A
25. A

TEST 2

DIRECTIONS: Each question or incomplete statement is followed by several suggested answers or completions. Select the one that BEST answers the question or completes the statement. *PRINT THE LETTER OF THE CORRECT ANSWER IN THE SPACE AT THE RIGHT.*

1. There are various forms of discovery that can be requested by either party in a lawsuit.
 _____ is the form of discovery that consists of written questions that are answered in writing and under oath.
     A. Depositions
     B. Examinations before trial
     C. Interrogatories
     D. Affidavits

2. At what point in a trial are jury instructions delivered by the judge?
     A. Before the trial begins
     B. After opening arguments
     C. After the defense rests
     D. Before the jury is to begin deliberations

3. In a bench trial, the _____ serves as the fact finder.
     A. jury   B. judge   C. bailiff   D. law clerk

4. The role of the bankruptcy trustee is to represent the
     A. interests of the bankruptcy estate and the creditors of the debtor
     B. debtor against all creditors
     C. largest creditor of the debtor
     D. small creditor of the debtor

5. The bankruptcy estate typically includes _____ at the time of filing.
     A. all property of the debtor, including interests in real property
     B. the home where the debtor resides
     C. the home and personal vehicle of the debtor
     D. all personal property, but not real property, of the debtor

6. An amicus curiae brief is filed by a person or entity with a(n) _____ in, but that is not a _____ in the case.
     A. outcome; party
     B. interest; party
     C. party; outcome
     D. party; interest

7. An answer is a formal response to which document?
     A. Deposition   B. Discovery   C. Complaint   D. Advice

8. Donovan sued his former employer, Ink Securities, LLC and his former boss, Steve, for unpaid wages. Ink Securities lost the case and now wishes to appeal the ruling.
 When Steve and Ink Securities, LLC appeal the case, what do they become?
     A. Appellees   B. Appellants   C. Plaintiffs   D. Defendants

9. In an indictment or information, each count represents a(n)
   A. proven crime
   B. request by the court
   C. decision on the merits
   D. allegation

10. Allison is sentenced to six years for armed robbery and ten years for grand larceny. She is sentenced to serve her prison terms concurrently. What is the MAXIMUM amount of time Allison will spend behind bars?
    A. Six years
    B. Sixteen years
    C. Ten years
    D. Four years

11. An appellate review de novo is one that provides no _____ to the ruling of the trial judge.
    A. deference
    B. credibility
    C. assignability
    D. advancement

12. Mary Ellen's house is worth $700,000, her car is worth $10,000, and she has cash and other financial assets worth $50,000. Creditors in Mary Ellen's bankruptcy have secured an interest in Mary Ellen's personal and real property amounting to $650,000.
    How much equity remains in Mary Ellen's property?
    A. $90,000
    B. $50,000
    C. $10,000
    D. $110,000

13. Ex parte communications are generally strictly forbidden because the
    A. other party is not privy to the information that is shared, creating the appearance of bias in a case
    B. associated cost to appeal a case with ex parte communications is an undue burden to the plaintiff
    C. defendant usually prevails when ex parte communications occur
    D. jury is not privy to the information that is shared, creating the appearance of bias in a case

14. What does the exclusionary rule exclude in a criminal trial?
    A. Testimony that is deemed hearsay by a judge in a court of competent jurisdiction
    B. Evidence obtained in violation of a defendant's constitutional or statutory rights
    C. Depositions that are unsworn or not notarized
    D. Affidavits that are unsworn or not notarized

15. Grand juries convene to determine whether there is _____ to believe an individual committed an offense.
    A. burden of proof
    B. reasonable belief
    C. probable cause
    D. an absolute determination

16. A liquidated claim is a claim that can be satisfied by
    A. a fixed amount of money
    B. real property
    C. personal property
    D. a percentage of property that will be sold

17. A motion to lift the automatic stay is a request to take action in a bankruptcy case that would otherwise violate the automatic stay.
    This motion is filed by the
    A. debtor's attorney
    B. bankruptcy trustee
    C. creditor(s)
    D. trustee's attorney

18. David is being arraigned and needs to enter a plea for the crime he allegedly committed while he was with his friend, Robert. Robert pleaded guilty during his arraignment yesterday, but David has been advised by his attorney to plead no contest, also known as
    A. nolo contendere
    B. pro se
    C. quid pro quo
    D. qui tam

19. Under federal law, a petty offense is any misdemeanor which is punishable by a period of _____ or less, a fine of not more than $5,000, or both.
    A. one year
    B. six months
    C. two years
    D. 1 month

20. If a case is remanded by a Court of Appeals, what effect does this have on the case at bar?
    A. The attorneys on the case are replaced for both the plaintiff and defendant.
    B. The appellant becomes the appellee in a new trial.
    C. The case is sent back to the trial, or lower, court.
    D. The trial court has the right to enter a determination to the Court of Appeals which may materially affect the outcome of the case.

21. Sentencing Guidelines are set by which entity or government entity?
    A. The Bureau of Prisons
    B. Immigration and Customs Enforcement
    C. Department of Justice
    D. U.S. Sentencing Commission

22. Sequestered juries are prevented from
    A. being biased by outside influences during deliberations
    B. speaking with one another during deliberations
    C. relying on alternate juror votes in rendering a decision in a trial
    D. hearing testimony from witnesses deemed to have hearsay evidence

23. A statute is a law passed by the
    A. courts
    B. judicial branch
    C. legislature
    D. executive branch

24. If an element or issue in a case has not arisen, or no longer applies to the matter at hand because it has ended before trial, the issue is considered
    A. triable
    B. factual
    C. indeterminate
    D. moot

25. Susan would like to file a restraining order on her ex-husband, John, and 25.____
may want to sue him criminally and civilly. She asks for advice on the rules of
conducting a lawsuit.
These rules are otherwise known as
   A. procedure   B. terms   C. requirements D. issues

KEY (CORRECT ANSWERS)

1.	C	11.	A
2.	D	12.	D
3.	B	13.	A
4.	A	14.	B
5.	A	15.	C
6.	B	16.	A
7.	C	17.	C
8.	B	18.	A
9.	D	19.	B
10.	C	20.	C

21.	D
22.	A
23.	C
24.	D
25.	A

TEST 3

DIRECTIONS: Each question or incomplete statement is followed by several suggested answers or completions. Select the one that BEST answers the question or completes the statement. *PRINT THE LETTER OF THE CORRECT ANSWER IN THE SPACE AT THE RIGHT.*

1. The delivery of writs or summons to one party in a lawsuit is also known as
   A. demand for interrogatories
   B. requests for information
   C. service of process
   D. statement on the record

   1.____

2. The time in which a lawsuit must be filed or a criminal prosecution must begin is called
   A. tolling period
   B. statute of limitations
   C. timely prosecution
   D. Article III hearing

   2.____

3. A subpoena requires its recipient to appear and provide _____, while a subpoena duces tecum requires its recipient to appear and provide _____.
   A. documents; testimony
   B. a witness; testimony
   C. documents; a witness
   D. testimony; documents

   3.____

4. _____ is the process of selecting a jury by questioning prospective jurors to ascertain their qualifications and determine if there is a basis for challenge, such as a conflict or other reason for disqualification.
   A. sua sponte
   B. de jure
   C. voir dire
   D. jury statement

   4.____

5. In executing a warrant, law enforcement has court authorization to make an arrest, _____, or both.
   A. conduct a search
   B. question a suspect
   C. subpoena a suspect's attorney
   D. require a personal appearance by the suspect

   5.____

6. A Chapter 7 case where there are no available assets of the debtor that would satisfy any portion of a creditor's unsecured claims is referred to as a(n)
   A. liquidation case
   B. no asset case
   C. unranked estate
   D. dischargeable debt

   6.____

7. Bill and Tim are neighbors. They are currently engaged in a heated dispute over the boundary of the property line that separates their lots. Bill has sued Tim for harassment as he claims Tim parks his delivery truck in the driveway that is on Bill's property. A judge has issued a court order which prevents Tim from parking any vehicle in the driveway in dispute until further research can be completed by the attorneys for either side.
   The court order issued is
   A. injunction
   B. restraining order
   C. issue
   D. home confinement

   7.____

8. If a case is dismissed without prejudice, that court has made no decision on the merits and the parties are allowed to
   A. question the final ruling
   B. file the case at a later date
   C. find new attorneys/representation
   D. ignore the final ruling

   8.____

9. May a deposition be used later in trial?
   A. Yes, but only if the witness was represented by an attorney
   B. Yes, as it is an oral statement made before an officer authorized by law to administer oaths
   C. No, because it is a written statement that can be retracted at any time
   D. No

   9.____

10. Madeline asks for advice regarding the discovery process. She is unsure what it entails.
    Discovery is the
    A. procedure that governs the exchange of information, particularly the disclosure of evidence, between the parties before trial
    B. procedure that governs the appearance of the testifying witnesses at trial
    C. rules of evidence both parties must adhere to during the trial
    D. exchange of motions and subpoenas before trial

    10.____

11. The docket is an important component of court proceedings because
    A. it is a log containing the complete history of each case
    B. it is accessible to the jury who can better understand the procedural history of each case.
    C. the judge enters the journal entries guaranteeing the docket's accuracy
    D. each court docket is at least 100 separate entries

    11.____

12. Information presented in testimony or in documents used to persuade a judge or jury in deciding a case in favor of one side or the other is termed
    A. disclosure   B. deposition   C. evidence   D. indictment

    12.____

13. Samuel is on trial for armed robbery. Samuel's attorney, Maxine, presents evidence her client was not in the state during the robbery and does not own a weapon of any kind.
    What kind of evidence is Maxine presenting to the court?
    A. Alibi   B. Exculpatory
    C. Exclusionary   D. Exemplary

    13.____

14. Samantha and Steven are separately called as witnesses in the trial of Adam Jones, who is being tried for murder. Steven testifies that he saw Adam commit the crime behind a local bar. Samantha testifies that Steven told her what Adam did.
    Adam's attorney objects to Samantha's testimony because it is
    A. exculpatory   B. hearsay
    C. untrue   D. impeachment

    14.____

15. After filing bankruptcy, Katherine sells her home to her daughter. Katherine's home is currently worth $300,000. She sells it to her daughter for $5. Katherine's sale of her home is deemed a
    A. insider transaction
    B. joint administration
    C. transfer of jurisprudence
    D. fraudulent transfer

16. When a trial is deemed invalid and must start again with a new jury, the trial is called a
    A. acquittal   B. mistrial   C. in limine   D. no asset case

17. Oral arguments are an opportunity for _____ to summarize their position before the court.
    A. jurors   B. plaintiffs   C. the accused   D. attorneys

18. During jury selection, the judge grants each side the right to exclude a certain number of prospective jurors without reason.
    This grant is also called a _____ challenge.
    A. prospective   B. per curiam   C. peremptory   D. petition

19. Who prepares the pre-sentence report for the court?
    A. The plaintiff's attorney
    B. The jury
    c. The defendant's attorney
    D. The court's probation officer

20. The legal doctrine that allows for the delay or pausing of the statute of limitations is referred to as
    A. extended delay
    B. tolling
    C. transferring
    D. tort

21. At trial, William was convicted of harassment and the negligent infliction of emotional distress. His attorney appealed the decision to the Court of Appeals. The Court of Appeals disagreed with the lower court and acquitted William of all charges.
    The Court of Appeals _____ the lower court's decision.
    A. remanded   b. reversed   C. returned   D. rescinded

22. The preparation of schedules requires the disclosure of
    A. assets, liabilities, and other financial information
    B. past convicted crimes
    C. past arrests
    D. past employment

23. The punishment ordered by a court for a defendant convicted of a crime is logged in the docket as the official
    A. disposition of the case
    B. sentence
    C. dismissal of the case
    D. order

24. John's trial is set to begin a month before Judge Smith. In a pre-trial hearing, it is determined that John is not a resident of the state where the trial will take place, and the alleged crime was not committed in the state. Judge Smith quickly realizes the court does not have jurisdiction and dismisses the case so that it can be filed with a court of proper jurisdiction.
Judge Smith's action, without prompting from either the plaintiff or defendant, is referred to as
   A. per diem   B. pro tem   C. sua sponte   D. en banc

25. In criminal cases, prosecutors must prove a defendant's guilt beyond a reasonable doubt.
In most civil trials, the _____ is by a preponderance of the evidence.
   A. clear and convincing
   B. standard of proof
   C. evidence
   D. degree and necessity

KEY (CORRECT ANSWERS)

1.	C	11.	A
2.	B	12.	C
3.	D	13.	B
4.	C	14.	B
5.	A	15.	D
6.	B	16.	B
7.	A	17.	D
8.	B	18.	C
9.	B	19.	D
10.	A	20.	B

21.	B
22.	A
23.	B
24.	C
25.	B

TEST 4

DIRECTIONS: Each question or incomplete statement is followed by several suggested answers or completions. Select the one that BEST answers the question or completes the statement. *PRINT THE LETTER OF THE CORRECT ANSWER IN THE SPACE AT THE RIGHT.*

1. The _____ is the final decision by the fact finder (judge or jury) that determines the guilt or innocence of a criminal defendant, or the outcome of a civil case.
    A. order
    B. punishment
    C. verdict
    D. decision

    1._____

2. Following precedent, or adhering to the decisions in prior cases involving the same issue is known as _____, the Latin term meaning "to stand by things decided."
    A. pro tempura
    B. en banc
    C. stare decisis
    D. quid pro quo

    2._____

3. One of the largest areas of civil law, a _____ is a wrongful or illegal act which causes injury to another.
    A. criminal   B. tort   C. defendant   D. punitive

    3._____

4. Stacy wants to sue Bob, who sold her a used car last year. Stacy alleges that Bob knowingly sold her a stolen car. Stacy paid Bob $5,000 for the car and in exchange Bob provided her with the keys to the car and a coupon for four free oil changes. No other documents were exchanged between Bob and Stacy.
    What document would prove who the legal owner of the car truly is?
    A. A wobbler
    B. Disclosure statement
    C. Schedule of ownership
    D. Title

    4._____

5. Michelle walks into a local courthouse and demands to speak with the clerk. She is upset that her neighbor, Rich, has not picked up the leaves on his property all season. She feels strongly his failure to do so will drive property prices down and, additionally, the leaves keep blowing into her yard.
    The clerk informs Michelle that she is free to contact an attorney, but should know that she will not likely be able to proceed with a lawsuit because
    A. there is no cause of action
    B. the courts cannot force Rich to pick up his leaves or prevent the leaves from blowing onto Michelle's property
    C. the statute of limitations will pass by the time Michelle contacts an attorney
    D. punitive damages are not likely to be awarded, so filing a lawsuit will be frivolous

    5._____

6. Latin for a "guilty mind," this term is synonymous with "intent" and for some crimes, it must be present when the person committed the criminal act in order to be found guilty.
   A. Pro se B. Mens rea C. Pro tem D. En banc

   6._____

7. Compensatory damages are different from punitive damages in that: Compensatory damages
   A. are recovered for injury or economic loss, while punitive are awarded over and above compensatory damages for the purpose of punishment and to serve as a deterrent to others
   B. and punitive damages both make the injured party whole, but compensatory damages can be up to 10% more than the actual claim
   C. serve as a deterrent to others, while punitive damages are recovered for injury or economic loss
   D. are incurred from the moment the crime occurs, thereby accruing interest, whereas punitive damages are awarded in a lump sum

   7._____

8. Malfeasance is defined as doing something illegal or morally wrong, and is usually associated with a(n)
   A. abuse of authority committed by a public official
   B. torts committed in a public setting
   C. crimes that are punishable by one year or more in prison
   D. a crime committed by a judge, court officer, or registered attorney

   8._____

9. A title abstract search on a home would provide the researcher with a
   A. list of people who made bids to buy the property
   B. list of real estate agents who worked on selling the home as well as a list of real estate agents representing potential buyers of the home
   C. history of ownership that establishes the present state of a title
   D. history of individuals who lived in the home at one point in time

   9._____

10. A crime that can be classified as either a felony or a misdemeanor is often referred to as a
    A. deciding factor B. wobbler
    C. precedent D. information

    10._____

11. A formal response to a complaint that pleads for dismissal due to a lack of a legal basis for a lawsuit is called
    A. an answer B. an affidavit
    C. a motion in limine D. demurrer

    11._____

12. Administrative law concerns _____ agencies, such as the U.S. Department of Housing and Urban Development (HUD) or the U.S. Department of Education.
    A. government B. municipal
    C. administrative D. elected

    12._____

13. Daniel committed and is currently being sentenced for his involvement in an armed robbery. His attorney is seeking alternative sanctions given that Daniel was present during the commission of the crime, but did not actively participate.
    His attorney asks the court for
    A. alternative sanctions
    B. sentencing by statute
    C. diminished capacity
    D. demurrer

14. The attorney who appears in the permanent records or files of a case is known as the _____ unless he or she withdraws or is otherwise removed from the case.
    A. attorney of the case
    B. attorney of record
    C. attorney in time
    D. permanent attorney

15. Mark and Cindy are divorcing. Cindy did not request money for support from Mark prior to the final court hearing, therefore her rights to _____ are waived.
    A. child support
    B. compensatory damages
    C. punitive damages
    D. alimony

16. Attorneys for the plaintiff and the defendant agree that each side needs more time to conduct additional discovery before trial.
    The parties jointly request a(n)
    A. recess
    B. voir dire
    C. adjournment
    D. information

17. Instead of using a judge, amicable parties may decide to submit to _____ for a decision.
    A. adjudication
    B. arbitration
    C. meritorious decision
    D. jury trial

18. The first court appearance of a person accused of a crime, where he or she is advised of his or her rights is called a(n)
    A. plea meeting
    B. pretrial conference
    C. jury selection
    D. arraignment

19. Charlie is behind on his child support and alimony payments to his ex-wife, Miranda. The court garnishes his wages to satisfy the amount in _____ that is overdue and unpaid.
    A. arrears   B. damages   C. satisfaction   D. lien

20. Joel became aware that he was being sued by his former business partner when he was served with a verified complaint by a process server last May. Joel decided to ignore the complaint altogether and believed that, eventually, the lawsuit would go away.
    What is Joel's status in the suit?
    A. He owes his former business partner punitive damages, because he failed to respond or answer.
    B. He is a defendant that will be forced to go to trial to answer to the charges.
    C. He is in default as he failed to answer or respond to the plaintiff's claims.
    D. He is in limbo as he did not answer the complaint but the trial date has not yet been set.

20.____

21. The permanent home of a person is referred to as their _____; where a person can have many residences, they can only have one of these.
    A. domicile   B. address
    C. place of business   D. permanency

21.____

22. Missy has been paroled after serving 60 months of her 120-month prison sentence. Parole is effectively a release
    A. into the custody of a responsible person
    B. from incarceration after serving part of a sentence
    C. from incarceration after serving more than half or a majority of a sentence
    D. into the custody of a probation officer who will continue to monitor the individual indefinitely

22.____

23. A petitioner is also known as the _____ or the person starting the lawsuit.
    A. applicant   B. plaintiff   C. respondent   D. defendant

23.____

24. After learning more about the circumstances surrounding the alleged armed robbery committed by Justin and three of his friends, the state's prosecutor decides to replace the original armed robbery charge against Justin for conspiracy to commit a felony.
    The prosecutor asks the court grant her request to enter a
    A. new charge   B. substitute charge
    C. felonious charge   D. determination of guilt

24.____

25. At a pretrial hearing to determine the credibility of the state's expert witness, the witness appeared and gave testimony followed by oral arguments by both the plaintiff's attorney and the defendant's attorney. Following the conference, each party decided they would like to review the record of what was said during that hearing prior to the trial. There was a stenographer during the pretrial hearing.
    Each party needs to request a(n)
    A. docket   B. witness log   C. transcript   D. disclosure

25.____

KEY (CORRECT ANSWERS)

1.	C	11.	D
2.	C	12.	A
3.	B	13.	A
4.	D	14.	B
5.	A	15.	D
6.	B	16.	C
7.	A	17.	B
8.	A	18.	D
9.	C	19.	A
10.	B	20.	C

21. A
22. B
23. B
24. B
25. C

EXAMINATION SECTION
TEST 1

DIRECTIONS: Each question or incomplete statement is followed by several suggested answers or completions. Select the one that BEST answers the question or completes the statement. *PRINT THE LETTER OF THE CORRECT ANSWER IN THE SPACE AT THE RIGHT.*

Questions 1-50.

DIRECTIONS: Each of Questions 1 through 50 consists of a word in capital letters followed by four suggested meanings of the word. For each question, choose the word or phrase which means MOST NEARLY the same as the word in capital letters.

1. ABUT
    A. abandon   B. assist   C. border on   D. renounce

2. ABSCOND
    A. draw in   B. give up
    C. refrain from   D. deal off

3. BEQUEATH
    A. deaden   B. hand down   C. make sad   D. scold

4. BOGUS
    A. sad   B. false   C. shocking   D. stolen

5. CALAMITY
    A. disaster   B. female   C. insanity   D. patriot

6. COMPULSORY
    A. binding   B. ordinary   C. protected   D. ruling

7. CONSIGN
    A. agree with   B. benefit
    C. commit   D. drive down

8. DEBILITY
    A. failure   B. legality
    C. quality   D. weakness

9. DEFRAUD
    A. cheat   B. deny
    C. reveal   D. tie

10. DEPOSITION
    A. absence   B. publication
    C. removal   D. testimony

11. DOMICILE
    A. anger   B. dwelling
    C. tame   D. willing

1.___
2.___
3.___
4.___
5.___
6.___
7.___
8.___
9.___
10.___
11.___

12. HEARSAY
    A. selfish   B. serious   C. rumor   D. unlikely

13. HOMOGENEOUS
    A. human   B. racial   C. similar   D. unwise

14. ILLICIT
    A. understood   B. uneven   C. unkind   D. unlawful

15. LEDGER
    A. book of accounts   B. editor
    C. periodical   D. shelf

16. NARRATIVE
    A. gossip   B. natural   C. negative   D. story

17. PLAUSIBLE
    A. reasonable   B. respectful   C. responsible   D. rightful

18. RECIPIENT
    A. absentee   B. receiver   C. speaker   D. substitute

19. SUBSTANTIATE
    A. appear for   B. arrange
    C. confirm   D. combine

20. SURMISE
    A. aim   B. break   C. guess   D. order

21. ALTER EGO
    A. business partner   B. confidential friend
    C. guide   D. subconscious conflict

22. FOURTH ESTATE
    A. the aristocracy   B. the clergy
    C. the judiciary   D. the newspapers

23. IMPEACH
    A. accuse   B. find guilty
    C. remove   D. try

24. PROPENSITY
    A. dislike   B. helpfulness
    C. inclination   D. supervision

25. SPLENETIC
    A. charming   B. peevish   C. shining   D. sluggish

26. SUBORN
    A. bribe someone to commit perjury
    B. demote someone several levels in rank
    C. deride
    D. substitute

27. TALISMAN
    A. charm
    B. juror
    C. prayer shawl
    D. native

28. VITREOUS
    A. corroding
    B. glassy
    C. nourishing
    D. sticky

29. WRY
    A. comic
    B. grained
    C. resilient
    D. twisted

30. SIGNATORY
    A. lawyer who draws up a legal document
    B. document that must be signed by a judge
    C. person who signs a document
    D. true copy of a signature

31. RETAINER
    A. fee paid to a lawyer for his services
    B. document held by a third party
    C. court decision to send a prisoner back to custody pending trial
    D. legal requirement to keep certain types of files

32. BEQUEATH
    A. to receive assistance from a charitable organization
    B. to give personal property by will to another
    C. to transfer real property from one person to another
    D. to receive an inheritance upon the death of a relative

33. RATIFY
    A. approve and sanction
    B. forego
    C. produce evidence
    D. summarize

34. CODICIL
    A. document introduced in evidence in a civil action
    B. subsection of a law
    C. type of legal action that can be brought by a plaintiff
    D. supplement or an addition to a will

35. ALIAS
    A. assumed name
    B. in favor of
    C. against
    D. a writ

36. PROXY
    A. a phony document in a real estate transaction
    B. an opinion by a judge of a civil court
    C. a document containing appointment of an agent
    D. a summons in a lawsuit

37. ALLEGED
    A. innocent
    B. asserted
    C. guilty
    D. called upon

38. EXECUTE
    A. to complete a legal document by signing it
    B. to set requirements
    C. to render services to a duly elected executive of a municipality
    D. to initiate legal action such as a lawsuit

39. NOTARY PUBLIC
    A. lawyer who is running for public office
    B. judge who hears minor cases
    C. public officer, one of whose functions is to administer oaths
    D. lawyer who gives free legal services to persons unable to pay

40. WAIVE
    A. to disturb a calm state of affairs
    B. to knowingly renounce a right or claim
    C. to pardon someone for a minor fault
    D. to purposely mislead a person during an investigation

41. ARRAIGN
    A. to prevent an escape
    B. to defend a prisoner
    C. to verify a document
    D. to accuse in a court of law

42. VOLUNTARY
    A. by free choice   B. necessary
    C. important   D. by design

43. INJUNCTION
    A. act of prohibiting   B. process of inserting
    C. means of arbitrating   D. freedom of action

44. AMICABLE
    A. compelled   B. friendly
    C. unimportant   D. insignificant

45. CLOSED SHOP
    A. one that employs only members of a union
    B. one that employs union members and unaffiliated employees
    C. one that employs only employees with previous experience
    D. one that employs skilled and unskilled workers

46. ABDUCT
    A. lead   B. kidnap   C. sudden   D. worthless

47. BIAS
    A. ability   B. envy   C. prejudice   D. privilege

48. COERCE
    A. cancel   B. force   C. rescind   D. rugged

49. CONDONE
    A. combine   B. pardon   C. revive   D. spice

    49.___

50. CONSISTENCY
    A. bravery   B. readiness
    C. strain   D. uniformity

    50.___

KEY (CORRECT ANSWERS)

1. C	11. B	21. B	31. A	41. D
2. D	12. C	22. D	32. B	42. A
3. B	13. C	23. A	33. A	43. A
4. B	14. D	24. C	34. D	44. B
5. A	15. A	25. B	35. A	45. A
6. A	16. D	26. A	36. C	46. B
7. C	17. A	27. A	37. B	47. C
8. D	18. B	28. B	38. A	48. B
9. A	19. C	29. D	39. C	49. B
10. D	20. C	30. C	40. B	50. D

TEST 2

DIRECTIONS: Each question or incomplete statement is followed by several suggested answers or completions. Select the one that BEST answers the question or completes the statement. *PRINT THE LETTER OF THE CORRECT ANSWER IN THE SPACE AT THE RIGHT.*

1. In the sentence, *The prisoner was fractious when brought to the station house*, the word *fractious* means MOST NEARLY
    A. penitent
    B. talkative
    C. irascible
    D. broken-hearted

2. In the sentence, *The judge was implacable when the attorney pleaded for leniency*, the word *implacable* means MOST NEARLY
    A. inexorable
    B. disinterested
    C. inattentive
    D. indifferent

3. In the sentence, *The court ordered the mendacious statements stricken from the record*, the word *mendacious* means MOST NEARLY
    A. begging
    B. lying
    C. threatening
    D. lengthy

4. In the sentence, *The district attorney spoke in a strident voice*, the word *strident* means MOST NEARLY
    A. loud
    B. harsh-sounding
    C. sing-song
    D. low

5. In the sentence, *The speaker had a predilection for long sentences*, the word *predilection* means MOST NEARLY
    A. aversion
    B. talent
    C. propensity
    D. diffidence

6. A person who has an uncontrollable desire to steal without need is called a
    A. dipsomaniac
    B. kleptomaniac
    C. monomaniac
    D. pyromaniac

7. In the sentence, *Malice was immanent in all his remarks*, the word *immanent* means MOST NEARLY
    A. elevated
    B. inherent
    C. threatening
    D. foreign

8. In the sentence, *The extant copies of the document were found in the safe*, the word *extant* means MOST NEARLY
    A. existing
    B. original
    C. forged
    D. duplicate

9. In the sentence, *The recruit was more complaisant after the captain spoke to him*, the word *complaisant* means MOST NEARLY
    A. calm
    B. affable
    C. irritable
    D. confident

10. In the sentence, *The man was captured under highly creditable circumstances*, the word *creditable* means MOST NEARLY
    A. doubtful
    B. believable
    C. praiseworthy
    D. unexpected

11. In the sentence, *His superior officers were more sagacious than he*, the word *sagacious* means MOST NEARLY
    A. shrewd
    B. obtuse
    C. absurd
    D. verbose

12. In the sentence, *He spoke with impunity*, the word *impunity* means MOST NEARLY
    A. rashness
    B. caution
    C. without fear
    D. immunity

13. In the sentence, *The new officer displayed unusual temerity during the emergency*, the word *temerity* means MOST NEARLY
    A. fear
    B. rashness
    C. calmness
    D. anxiety

14. In the sentence, *The portions of food were parsimoniously served*, the word *parsimoniously* means MOST NEARLY
    A. stingily
    B. piously
    C. elaborately
    D. generously

15. In the sentence, *Generally the speaker's remarks were sententious*, the word *sententious* means MOST NEARLY
    A. verbose
    B. witty
    C. argumentative
    D. pithy

Questions 16-20.

DIRECTIONS: Next to the number which corresponds with the number of each item in Column I, place the letter preceding the adjective in Column II which BEST describes the persons in Column I.

COLUMN I	COLUMN II
16. Talkative woman	A. abstemious
17. Person on a reducing diet	B. pompous
18. Scholarly professor	C. erudite
19. Man who seldom speaks	D. benevolent
20. Charitable person	E. docile
	F. loquacious
	G. indefatigable
	H. taciturn

Questions 21-25.

DIRECTIONS: Next to the number which corresponds with the number preceding each profession in Column I, place the letter preceding the word in Column II which BEST explains the subject matter of that profession.

COLUMN I	COLUMN II	
21. Geologist	A. animals	21. ___
22. Oculist	B. eyes	22. ___
23. Podiatrist	C. feet	23. ___
24. Palmist	D. fortune-telling	24. ___
25. Zoologist	E. language	25. ___
	F. rocks	
	G. stamps	
	H. woman	

Questions 26-30.

DIRECTIONS: Next to the number corresponding to the number of each of the words in Column I, place the letter preceding the word in Column II that is MOST NEARLY OPPOSITE to it in meaning.

COLUMN I	COLUMN II	
26. comely	A. beautiful	26. ___
27. eminent	B. cowardly	27. ___
28. frugal	C. kind	28. ___
29. gullible	D. sedate	29. ___
30. valiant	E. shrewd	30. ___
	F. ugly	
	G. unknown	
	H. wasteful	

KEY (CORRECT ANSWERS)

1.	C	11.	A	21.	F
2.	A	12.	D	22.	B
3.	B	13.	B	23.	C
4.	B	14.	A	24.	D
5.	C	15.	D	25.	A
6.	B	16.	F	26.	F
7.	B	17.	A	27.	G
8.	A	18.	C	28.	H
9.	B	19.	H	29.	E
10.	C	20.	D	30.	B

VOCABULARY EXAMINATION SECTION
TEST 1

DIRECTIONS: In each of the following questions, select the lettered word or phrase which means MOST NEARLY the same as the word in capital letters. *PRINT THE LETTER OF THE CORRECT ANSWER IN THE SPACE AT THE RIGHT.*

1. INTERROGATE   1.____
    A. question   B. arrest   C. search   D. rebuff

2. PERVERSE   2.____
    A. manageable   B. poetic
    C. contrary   D. patient

3. ADVOCATE   3.____
    A. champion   B. employ   C. select   D. advise

4. APPARENT   4.____
    A. desirable   B. clear   C. partial   D. possible

5. INSINUATE   5.____
    A. survey   B. strengthen
    C. suggest   D. insist

6. MOMENTOUS   6.____
    A. important   B. immediate C. delayed   D. short

7. AUXILIARY   7.____
    A. exciting   B. assisting C. upsetting D. available

8. ADMONISH   8.____
    A. praise   B. increase   C. warn   D. polish

9. ANTICIPATE   9.____
    A. agree   B. expect   C. conceal   D. approve

10. APPREHEND   10.____
    A. confuse   B. sentence   C. release   D. seize

11. CLEMENCY   11.____
    A. silence   B. freedom   C. mercy   D. severity

12. THWART   12.____
    A. enrage   B. strike   C. choke   D. block

13. RELINQUISH   13.____
    A. stretch   B. give up   C. weaken   D. flee from

107

14. CURTAIL
    A. stop B. reduce C. repair D. insult

15. INACCESSIBLE
    A. obstinate B. unreachable
    C. unreasonable D. puzzling

16. PERTINENT
    A. related B. saucy C. durable D. impatient

17. INTIMIDATE
    A. encourage B. hunt C. beat D. frighten

18. INTEGRITY
    A. honesty B. wisdom
    C. understanding D. persistence

19. UTILIZE
    A. use B. manufacture
    C. help D. include

20. SUPPLEMENT
    A. regulate B. demand C. add D. answer

21. INDISPENSABLE
    A. essential B. neglected
    C. truthful D. unnecessary

22. ATTAIN
    A. introduce B. spoil C. achieve D. study

23. PRECEDE
    A. break away B. go ahead
    C. begin D. come before

24. HAZARD
    A. penalty B. adventure
    C. handicap D. danger

25. DETRIMENTAL
    A. uncertain B. harmful C. fierce D. horrible

KEY (CORRECT ANSWERS)

1.	A	11.	C
2.	C	12.	D
3.	A	13.	B
4.	B	14.	B
5.	C	15.	B
6.	A	16.	A
7.	B	17.	D
8.	C	18.	A
9.	B	19.	A
10.	D	20.	C

21. A
22. C
23. D
24. D
25. B

TEST 2

DIRECTIONS: In each of the following questions, select the lettered word or phrase which means MOST NEARLY the same as the word in capital letters. *PRINT THE LETTER OF THE CORRECT ANSWER IN THE SPACE AT THE RIGHT.*

1. AVARICE
   A. flight   B. greed   C. pride   D. thrift

   1.____

2. PREDATORY
   A. offensive   B. plundering
   C. previous   D. timeless

   2.____

3. VINDICATE
   A. clear   B. conquer   C. correct   D. illustrate

   3.____

4. INVETERATE
   A. backward   B. erect   C. habitual   D. lucky

   4.____

5. DISCERN
   A. describe   B. fabricate   C. recognize   D. seek

   5.____

6. COMPLACENT
   A. indulgent   B. listless   C. overjoyed   D. satisfied

   6.____

7. ILLICIT
   A. insecure   B. unclear   C. unlawful   D. unlimited

   7.____

8. PROCRASTINATE
   A. declare   B. multiply   C. postpone   D. steal

   8.____

9. IMPASSIVE
   A. calm   B. frustrated
   C. thoughtful   D. unhappy

   9.____

10. AMICABLE
    A. cheerful   B. flexible   C. friendly   D. poised

    10.____

11. FEASIBLE
    A. breakable   B. easy
    C. likeable   D. practicable

    11.____

12. INNOCUOUS
    A. armless   B. insecure   C. insincere   D. unfavorable

    12.____

13. OSTENSIBLE
    A. apparent   B. hesitant   C. reluctant   D. showy

    13.____

110

14. INDOMITABLE 14.____
    A. excessive   B. unconquerable
    C. unreasonable   D. unthinkable

15. CRAVEN 15.____
    A. cowardly   B. hidden   C. miserly   D. needed

16. ALLAY 16.____
    A. discuss   B. quiet   C. refine   D. remove

17. ALLUDE 17.____
    A. denounce   B. refer   C. state   D. support

18. NEGLIGENCE 18.____
    A. carelessness   B. denial
    C. objection   D. refusal

19. AMEND 19.____
    A. correct   B. destroy   C. end   D. list

20. RELEVANT 20.____
    A. conclusive   B. careful
    C. obvious   D. related

21. VERIFY 21.____
    A. challenge   B. change   C. confirm   D. reveal

22. INSIGNIFICANT 22.____
    A. incorrect   B. limited
    C. unimportant   D. undesirable

23. SCURRILOUS 23.____
    A. hideous   B. abusive   C. dirty   D. illegal

24. PERPETRATE 24.____
    A. indefinite   B. harass
    C. solicit   D. commit

25. AMORPHOUS 25.____
    A. shapeless   B. loving
    C. debt-ridden   D. indecent

KEY (CORRECT ANSWERS)

1.	B	11.	D
2.	B	12.	A
3.	A	13.	A
4.	C	14.	B
5.	C	15.	A
6.	D	16.	B
7.	C	17.	B
8.	C	18.	A
9.	A	19.	A
10.	C	20.	D

21. C
22. C
23. B
24. D
25. A

TEST 3

DIRECTIONS: In each of the following questions, select the lettered word or phrase which means MOST NEARLY the same as the word in capital letters. *PRINT THE LETTER OF THE CORRECT ANSWER IN THE SPACE AT THE RIGHT.*

1. IMPLY
   - A. agree to
   - B. hint at
   - C. laugh at
   - D. mimic
   - E. reduce

   1.____

2. APPRAISAL
   - A. allowance
   - B. composition
   - C. prohibition
   - D. quantity
   - E. valuation

   2.____

3. DISBURSE
   - A. approve
   - B. expend
   - C. prevent
   - D. relay
   - E. restrict

   3.____

4. POSTERITY
   - A. back payment
   - B. current procedure
   - C. final effort
   - D. future generations
   - E. rare specimen

   4.____

5. PUNCTUAL
   - A. clear
   - B. honest
   - C. polite
   - D. prompt
   - E. prudent

   5.____

6. PRECARIOUS
   - A. abundant
   - B. alarmed
   - C. cautious
   - D. insecure
   - E. placid

   6.____

7. FOSTER
   - A. delegate
   - B. demote
   - C. encourage
   - D. plead
   - E. surround

   7.____

8. PINNACLE
   - A. center
   - B. crisis
   - C. outcome
   - D. peak
   - E. personification

   8.____

9. COMPONENT
   - A. flattery
   - B. opposite
   - C. part
   - D. revision
   - E. trend

   9.____

10. SOLICIT
    - A. ask
    - B. prohibit
    - C. promise
    - D. revoke
    - E. surprise

    10.____

11. LIAISON
    - A. asset
    - B. coordination
    - C. difference
    - D. policy
    - E. procedure

    11.____

12. ALLEGE

    A. assert   B. break   C. irritate
    D. reduce   E. wait

13. INFILTRATION

    A. consumption   B. disposal   C. enforcement
    D. penetration   E. seizure

14. SALVAGE

    A. announce   B. combine   C. prolong
    D. save   E. try

15. MOTIVE

    A. attack   B. favor   C. incentive
    D. patience   E. tribute

16. PROVOKE

    A. adjust   B. incite   C. leave
    D. obtain   E. practice

17. SURGE

    A. branch   B. contract   C. revenge
    D. rush   E. want

18. MAGNIFY

    A. attract   B. demand   C. generate
    D. increase   E. puzzle

19. PREPONDERANCE

    A. decision   B. judgment   C. outweighing
    D. submission E. warning

20. ABATE

    A. assist   B. coerce   C. diminish
    D. indulge   E. trade

KEY (CORRECT ANSWERS)

1.	B	11.	B
2.	E	12.	A
3.	B	13.	D
4.	D	14.	D
5.	D	15.	C
6.	D	16.	B
7.	C	17.	D
8.	D	18.	D
9.	C	19.	C
10.	A	20.	C

TEST 4

DIRECTIONS: In each of the following questions, select the lettered word or phrase which means MOST NEARLY the same as, or the opposite of, the word in capital letters. *PRINT THE LETTER OF THE CORRECT ANSWER IN THE SPACE AT THE RIGHT.*

1. VINDICTIVE
    - A. centrifugal
    - B. forgiving
    - C. molten
    - D. tedious
    - E. vivacious

2. SCOPE
    - A. compact
    - B. detriment
    - C. facsimile
    - D. potable
    - E. range

3. HINDER
    - A. amplify
    - B. aver
    - C. method
    - D. observe
    - E. retard

4. IRATE
    - A. adhere
    - B. angry
    - C. authentic
    - D. peremptory
    - E. vacillate

5. APATHY
    - A. accessory
    - B. availability
    - C. fervor
    - D. pacify
    - E. stride

6. LUCRATIVE
    - A. effective
    - B. imperfect
    - C. injurious
    - D. timely
    - E. worthless

7. DIVERSITY
    - A. convection
    - B. slip
    - C. temerity
    - D. uniformity
    - E. viscosity

8. OVERT
    - A. laugh
    - B. lighter
    - C. orifice
    - D. quay
    - E. sly

9. SPORADIC
    - A. divide
    - B. incumbrance
    - C. livid
    - D. occasional
    - E. original

10. RESCIND
    - A. annul
    - B. deride
    - C. extol
    - D. indulge
    - E. insist

11. AUGMENT
    - A. alter
    - B. decrease
    - C. obey
    - D. perceive
    - E. supersede

12. AUTONOMOUS   12._____
    A. careless   B. conceptual   C. constant
    D. defamatory   E. independent

13. TRANSCRIPT   13._____
    A. copy   B. report   C. sentence
    D. termination   E. verdict

14. DISCORDANT   14._____
    A. astride   B. comprised   C. effusive
    D. harmonious   E. slick

15. DISTEND   15._____
    A. constrict   B. direct   C. redeem
    D. silence   E. submerge

16. EMANATE   16._____
    A. bridge   B. coherency   C. conquer
    D. degrade   E. flow

17. EXULTANT   17._____
    A. easily upset   B. in bad taste
    C. in high spirits   D. subject to moods
    E. very much over-priced

18. PREVARICATE   18._____
    A. hesitate   B. increase   C. lie
    D. procrastinate   E. reject

19. COGNIZANT   19._____
    A. obvious   B. search   C. stupid
    D. suspicious   E. unaware

20. CREDIBLE   20._____
    A. daring   B. helpful   C. surreptitious
    D. unbelievable   E. uncontrollable

KEY (CORRECT ANSWERS)

1. B
2. E
3. E
4. B
5. C

6. E
7. D
8. E
9. D
10. A

11. B
12. E
13. A
14. D
15. A

16. E
17. C
18. C
19. E
20. D

EXAMINATION SECTION
TEST 1

DIRECTIONS: In each of the following groups, one of the four sentences contains an error in grammar, usage, diction, or punctuation. Indicate the INCORRECT sentence. *PRINT THE LETTER OF THE CORRECT ANSWER IN THE SPACE AT THE RIGHT.*

1. A. After shaking hands with me, he said, "You're most welcome, I assure you." 1.____
    B. He exclaimed, "What a mistake you have made!" upon hearing my account of the discussion.
    C. What is meant by "Dog eat dog"?
    D. "I'd like to travel all over the world," said the young man; just to see how the 'other half' lives, you know."

2. A. During the lecture, the speaker was repeatedly disturbed by the shouts of the small boys on the streets. 2.____
    B. The injured woman having been given first aid, we offered to take her to the nearest hospital.
    C. Due to the continued rain and wind, we have been unable to leave the house for several days.
    D. I could not respect him as I do if he were not upright and honest.

3. A. This is John, Tom and Harry's room. 3.____
    B. John borrowed his brother-in-law's car.
    C. The department store is advertising a sale of mens' clothing.
    D. Who shall I say telephoned?

4. A. My friend Harris lives in Brooklyn. 4.____
    B. Between each period, teachers must stand in the corridor to direct traffic.
    C. The committee proposed that he be dropped from the organization.
    D. Only within the past few months have I begun to know her.

5. A. Hoping for the best is not as effective as to work hard. 5.____
    B. Set it down on the desk.
    C. I insist that he accompany me.
    D. School over at last, they ran to their games.

6. A. The class had no sooner become interested in the lesson than the bell rang. 6.____
    B. At that time, I was especially desirous to make her acquaintance.
    C. The tearful parents were oblivious of everyone else but their daughter.
    D. Florence's skill on the instrument was conceded to be unsurpassed in the school.

7. A. Of the two plans described, the second is the most important. 7.____
    B. A two weeks' vacation is necessary after a hard year's work.
    C. On June first, our neighbors will have been living in the same house for thirty years.
    D. Everybody who has paid the full purchase price should call for his set of books now.

8. A. It was superior in every way to the book previously used.
    B. His testimony today is different from that of yesterday.
    C. If you would have studied the problem carefully, you would have found the solution more quickly.
    D. The flowers smelled so sweet that the whole house was perfumed.

9. A. Next summer I shall either travel by plane or by boat down to Bermuda.
    A. May we infer then that you were really just an innocent bystander?
    B. Undoubtedly the best scene in the play occurs when the son confronts his mother.
    C. History is the record of events that have happened.

10. A. The leader, with all his scores of followers, was arrested.
    B. Howard is a friend of my brother.
    C. Jerry never has and never will do a good day's work.
    D. Did any of the applicants bring his tools?

11. A. His speed was equal to that of a racehorse.
    B. His failure was due to weak eyes.
    C. The reason I am late is because I was sick.
    D. Of course, my opinion is worth less than a lawyer's.

12. A. The winters were hard and dreary, nothing could live without shelter.
    B. Not one in a thousand readers takes the matter seriously.
    C. Every candidate except my friend and me seems to know exactly how to relax.
    D. If I had known that it was you, I should have acted differently.

13. A. The social activities of college life were his sole interest.
    B. After hearing modern jazz, all other music sounds dull.
    C. Surely there can be no objection to their working on a volunteer basis.
    D. Favored by a warm climate, Florida is a popular resort.

14. A. This will not be easy for me, I being without experience.
    B. He said that he had been here before and that he expected to return.
    C. He is not so competent as we thought him to be.
    D. Since the installation of the traffic light, there have been less accidents at that crossing.

15. A. Besides her own family of four boys, my grandmother reared two adopted children.
    B. This kind of apples ripens earlier than any other in our section of the country.
    C. She was so kind to us girls when we were little children that we shall always be grateful to her.
    D. The invention of such amusements as the radio, television, and movies have probably influenced the habits of millions.

16. A. We still do not believe the thief to be him, in spite of the evidence to the contrary.
    B. These data, although very interesting, are not really significant.
    C. Every man, every woman, every child was interested in the program.
    D. He is one of the most able men who has ever been in the Senate.

17.
 A. The girl swum the Mississippi River.
 B. Price levels rose ten points last year.
 C. The freshmen were forbidden to speak to the sophomores.
 D. He was here when the boy brought the news.

17._____

18.
 A. The lines on the map are finely drawn.
 B. He spoke very slowly.
 C. The lady looked good in her new suit.
 D. The cream tasted sour.

18._____

19.
 A. The day is warm.
 B. It should be called to his attention.
 C. The girl was an unusually beautiful child.
 D. He performed the job easy and quick.

19._____

20.
 A. The company published its new catalogue last week.
 B. The man who he introduced was Mr. Carey.
 C. The Rolls-Royce is the fastest car in England.
 D. He finished the job satisfactorily.

20._____

21.
 A. The crew did its best to complete the job on time.
 B. They have already went home.
 C. The children drank some lemonade.
 D. The girl has written her composition.

21._____

22.
 A. She saw the letter laying here this morning.
 B. They gave the poor man some food when he knocked on the door.
 C. The plans were drawn before the fight started.
 D. He was here when the messenger brought the news.

22._____

23.
 A. I regret the loss caused by the error.
 B. The students will have a new teacher.
 C. It shall rain before the afternoon is over.
 D. They swore to bring out all the facts.

23._____

24.
 A. If my trip is a success, I should be back on Thursday.
 B. We will send a copy of the article to you if you wish it.
 C. They will have gone before the notice is sent to their office.
 D. Can I use this information in my speech?

24._____

25.
 A. He likes these kind of pencils better than those kind.
 B. That Jackson will be elected is evident.
 C. He does not approve of my dictating the letter.
 D. Jack should make some progress in his work each day.

25._____

26.
 A. The company has moved into its new building.
 B. They will approve him going to the concert.
 C. That business is good appears to be true.
 D. It was he who won the prize.

26._____

27.
- A. We will notify whomever you wish.
- B. I expect him this morning.
- C. If he lays down on the job, he will regret it.
- D. In the old records was found a queer mistake.

27._____

28.
- A. The manager's statement relating to the two letters is without doubt correct.
- B. Either you are the winner or I am.
- C. The mother knew where the little boy had hidden his toys.
- D. He has forgot where they bought the equipment.

28._____

29.
- A. He will study the lesson providing he can find his book.
- B. It looks as if they will come.
- C. The meeting of the committee was held in the Rose Room.
- D. He decided to open a branch store.

29._____

30.
- A. I wrote first and telephoned later.
- B. He should of taken the order.
- C. All our offices close on Saturday.
- D. Our principal business is selling.

30._____

31.
- A. Who shall I say called?
- B. The water has frozen the pipes.
- C. Everyone has left except them.
- D. Everyone of the salesmen must supply their own car.

31._____

32.
- A. The driver did all that it was possible to do.
- B. He agreed to phone you before now.
- C. I thought it to be he.
- D. We expected to stay there.

32._____

33.
- A. Two-thirds of the building is finished.
- B. Where are Mr. Keene and Mr. Herbert?
- C. Neither the floorwalker nor the salesladies want to work overtime.
- D. The committee was agreed.

33._____

34.
- A. Who did we give the order to?
- B. Send your order immediately.
- C. You will thrill at the beauty of the mountain.
- D. I believe I paid the bill.

34._____

35.
- A. Amends have been made for the damage to one of our cars.
- B. Neither the customer nor the clerk were aware of the fire in the store.
- C. A box of spare pencils is on the desk.
- D. There is the total number of missing pens.

35._____

36.
- A. The company insist on everyone's being prompt.
- B. Each one of our salesmen takes an aptitude test.
- C. It is the location that appeals to me.
- D. Most of the men have left the building.

36._____

37. A. We're sure she'll respond if your careful about the suggestions she's given each day.
    B. I have always been of the opinion that that kind of examination is of little value.
    C. The papers will not blow away if you lay the paper weight on them.
    D. He had scarcely finished his lines when the audience began to applaud wildly.

38. A. Modern furniture may be used for many purposes for which period furniture cannot.
    B. I had but five minutes to catch the train.
    C. He told Marjorie and me that he would not come.
    D. Each of the wheels on those trucks have twelve spokes.

39. A. No one knows the correct answer to that question except you and me.
    B. It looked like it was going to be a pleasant day, so we left our umbrellas at home.
    C. The judge said that punishment would be meted out to whomever deserved it.
    D. "*The words, 'Give me liberty or give me death*," he answered incorrectly but with assurance, "were said by Nathan Hale."

40. A. It is I who am mistaken.
    B. Is it John or Mary who stand at the head of the class?
    C. He is one of those pupils who always do their lessons.
    D. He is a man whom I can depend on in time of trouble.

41. A. At first glance, the old man believed him to be me.
    B. His failure to complete his work in college last term might have been due to his child's illness.
    C. The scenery in Banff is somewhat like Switzerland, although Banff is much farther north.
    D. Whatever your decision may be will be quite satisfactory, I am sure.

42. A. The children's plans for a surprise party had been made very quietly, but John's suspicions had been aroused.
    B. There must be some faraway place where one can spend a quiet holiday.
    C. Rather than crowd the page, it is preferable to leave a line blank between each word.
    D. I have never understood why a good facsimile should not be so valuable as an original.

43. A. He feels ill, but his sister looks worse.
    B. The Joneses are going to visit their friends in Chicago.
    C. ROBINSON CRUSOE, which is a fairy tale to the child, is a work of social philosophy to the mature thinker.
    D. I was appreciative of all his efforts, but especially of him doing that one job for me.

44. A. They have written to all of us-Harry, you, and I.
    B. That I am sick is no proof that I ate too much.
    C. In one of Sinclair Lewis's novels the clergy is satirized.
    D. At the fringe of the crowd, peering through all those bodies, stood Henry and I.

45.
- A. To enjoy a walking trip, take care that your feet are in good condition.
- B. One or the other of those fellows has stolen it.
- C. The man whom I thought was my friend deceived me.
- D. He said he thought he should ride.

46.
- A. The possession of certain skills and abilities are necessary for that type of work.
- B. The beautiful elm trees are in danger of being killed by a disease which was brought here from Europe.
- C. When you're in doubt about your best friend's loyalty, you can't help being disappointed.
- D. These data help to prove that his statements are well founded.

47.
- A. Are you much taller than I?
- B. She lived in the city for three years before she visited her aunt.
- C. He lay the book down on the table and angrily stalked out of the room.
- D. He read excerpts from his new novel to John and me.

48.
- A. The lilacs, the early roses, and the lush warmth of the morning smelled fragrant as odors from the gardens of Heaven.
- B. I found it to be fruitful to study the plan in detail, setting aside several items for daily consideration, the time depending upon the quantity of other work.
- C. Let's you and I confront him together.
- D. Maugham has the ability to hold his reader's attention.

49.
- A. The poem is somewhat longer than a sonnet; its rhythm is fittingly sedate.
- B. If they would have considered all the suggestions carefully, they would have come to a different conclusion.
- C. Among the plans submitted were many up-to-date ideas, some of which were adopted.
- D. When the toy balloon burst, the child screamed piercingly with fright.

50.
- A. Coming in on the train, the high school building is seen on the left.
- B. I shall relay the message to my secretary upon her arrival.
- C. She is a member of a literary group that meets regularly.
- D. They work nights independently of one another.

KEY (CORRECT ANSWERS)

1. D	11. C	21. B	31. D	41. C
2. C	12. A	22. A	32. C	42. C
3. C	13. B	23. C	33. C	43. D
4. B	14. D	24. D	34. A	44. A
5. A	15. D	25. A	35. B	45. C
6. B	16. D	26. B	36. A	46. A
7. A	17. A	27. C	37. A	47. C
8. C	18. C	28. D	38. D	48. C
9. A	19. D	29. A	39. D	49. B
10. C	20. B	30. B	40. B	50. A

TEST 2

DIRECTIONS: In each of the following groups, one of the four sentences contains an error in grammar, usage, diction, or punctuation. Indicate the INCORRECT sentence. *PRINT THE LETTER OF THE CORRECT ANSWER IN THE SPACE AT THE RIGHT.*

1. A. Had I remained at home, as my father advised, I should have heard the news as soon as you did.
   B. His normal health was soon restored to him by the balmy climate.
   C. He is very different in temperament than his brother.
   D. Does neither of them expect to attend the reception?

   1.____

2. A. It seems to be Ed who must do most of the work.
   B. John had interesting news for us; the meeting was still in session.
   C. Accident prevention is everybodys' concern every day in the week.
   D. Boys' and girls' furnishings are sold on the second floor.

   2.____

3. A. We planned to stay a week at Rocky Landing.
   B. The bus driver agreed to take as many as wanted to go.
   C. Any man may vote, be he rich or poor.
   D. The teacher assigned three of us, John, Sam, and I to help with the arrangements for the party.

   3.____

4. A. There are no lakes in Pennsylvania like they have in the central part of New York State.
   B. Waiting dejectedly at the door, he could give no explanation for his failure.
   C. There are hardly any people left in town who remember his boyhood.
   D. The entire city was aroused at the news of the general's killing himself.

   4.____

5. A. They really believed they were stronger than we.
   B. The one thing left was a quantity of broken tin cans.
   C. Who do you think will be chosen for the position by the superintendent?
   D. The coach, together with six or seven players, were quarreling heatedly with the referee.

   5.____

6. A. The whole class wanted the winner to be him.
   B. If he prepares carefully, he is liable to win the contest.
   C. Neither the two boys nor the only girl was chosen by the committee.
   D. There seem to be many people ready to apply for the position.

   6.____

7. A. His failure to prepare will probably mitigate against his possibility of success.
   B. Do you think that you could have swum all the way to the island?
   C. Although his lawyer objected, the prisoner was sentenced to be hanged next month.
   D. We have heard none of the details of the story.

   7.____

8. A. In this first matter although it appears simple, thereare probably going to be many   8._____
      statements of opinion.
   B. We believed him to be the best choice.
   C. While we waited, the interval between each stroke of the bell seemed to grow longer.
   D. What he saw was a company of men in a close group.

9. A. Disagreement, bickering, and quarreling is a frequent occurrence when that orga-   9._____
      nization holds its meetings.
   B. I felt bad when I saw the test results.
   C. The man's death was due to exposure to the cold.
   D. Everyone arrived on time except Smith, Brown, and him.

10. A. It's time you knew how to divide by two numbers.   10._____
    B. Are you sure the bell has rung?
    C. Whose going to prepare the lunch for the picnic?
    D. Will it be all right if you are called at ten o'clock?

11. A. Everybody, busy, lying in the sun, or carelessly looking on, considered himself one   11._____
       of the group.
    B. Unlike you or I, Joseph receives a large allowance each week.
    C. You may tell him our teacher is displeased.
    D. Whom do you believe to be the best athlete in the group?

12. A. When you go on a vacation trip be sure to take a supply of color film along with   12._____
       you.
    B. We are happy to read that there are higher wages today and less employed than
       ever before in our history.
    C. The principal will address the senior class on opportunities in teaching.
    D. Every available student, including the twenty-five freshmen in Mr. Smith's class,
       is invited to enter the contest.

13. A. When the test period ended, the teacher realized that he prepared a test that was   13._____
       much too difficult for the average pupil in the class.
    B. The agenda for our next meeting were prepared well ahead of the meeting.
    C. "One of the answers is correct," the teacher said: "you are to make the right
       choice."
    D. The New York State Commission for the Blind is preparing a fundraising cam-
       paign.

14. A. Interest, talent, and opportunity must be explored in sound vocational guidance.   14._____
    B. The person who from all points of view was the best leader was the one finally
       chosen.
    C. Whoever you like so well is always welcome at our house.
    D. When I realize how hard he worked, I feel bad.

15. A. Intending to reach home before dark, at six o'clock we began the trip at the   15._____
       entrance to the park.
    B. The most concrete criticism was the fact that he was disinterested in his studies.
    C. Laziness is responsible for a great many spelling errors.
    D. The new men's store advertised its opening sale day for Monday.

16. A. The management of traffic in our city, large as it is, compares favorably with any other city in the country.
    B. Should you ask for another book, I should be happy to help you find it.
    C. The candidate's real interest in securing the nomination no longer remaining in doubt, the politicians are backing him for the office.
    D. Never having known the man personally or socially, although they had worked together for years, the superintendent felt that he could not recommend him.

    16.____

17. A. Successfully to complete the assigned work is a first requirement for a good grade.
    B. All of us present in the auditorium agreed that it would be unwise to leave such severe criticism go without reply.
    C. None of the three hundred seniors was truly qualified for the new post.
    D. Owing to the intervention of an interested party, the business deal was successfully completed.

    17.____

18. A. There was no one but my best friend, John, and me still fishing after eight o'clock.
    B. He is one of those successful people who believes that achievement depends on hard work.
    C. How can you compare the taste of my pie with the flavor of her dessert?
    D. We were amazed at his choosing the last two weeks in July as his vacation.

    18.____

19. A. You tell him I'm not pleased with his work.
    B. They wandered all over the state as if they didn't know the route.
    C. Efficiency was introduced in all three stores, but like the first two, the third was soon in financial difficulties.
    D. He is the kind of man who impresses you, the first time he meets you.

    19.____

20. A. You may be sure that he is the same man whom you met on your first visit.
    B. Being that you arrived first, you will be given first choice of the available seats.
    C. In spite of his injury, he was selected to make the trip with the team.
    D. Either my friend or I am ready to write the answer to the last question.

    20.____

21. A. Five years are long enough to have stayed away from home.
    B. Do you think we are justified in answering their questions?
    C. Knowing that you are ready, the idea is very good for me to call you now.
    D. This is a wholly different problem from the one we solved yesterday.

    21.____

22. A. The boy looked like he had gone through a difficult period.
    B. During the game every one of the students is expected to cheer, to applaud, and to act like a sportsman.
    C. The opera finished, the audience cheered every performer.
    D. A series of biographical sketches is to be released soon.

    22.____

23. A. He, not you, is to lead the band.
    B. Beside Mr. Truman there is one other former president living.
    C. His decision to continue the search was the cause of the tragedy, it appears.
    D. The flower smells sweet after a chemical spraying.

    23.____

24. A. There is an increasing number of retarded readers in the ninth year.
    B. The pupil liked English better than biology, arithmetic, or Spanish.
    C. Many explanations are possible; perhaps poor health was the deciding factor.
    D. Many pupils seem to enjoy playing games alone but not to lose in these games.

    24.____

25.
   A. Every nation has their own problems to contend with.
   B. Speak to whoever is best able to give directions.
   C. The prize should be given to whomever the committee chooses.
   D. The farther you walk, the more lovely the road becomes.

25.____

26.
   A. The committee of councilmen is ready to act now.
   B. The parent, accompanied by his children, is to be shown into the room.
   C. Give the answer to whoever opens the door first.
   D. The investigation may be wise, but in my opinion I think it is not necessary.

26.____

27.
   A. Born in India and educated in England, Kipling's stories have the flavor of both countries.
   B. He had an accident in his sister-in-law's car.
   C. Practicing for many months, he learned to dance better than she.
   D. The teacher, together with his pupils, was late for the bus.

27.____

28.
   A. Think carefully before voting, because your's is the important decision.
   B. Whomever you decide upon, we shall accept your choice.
   C. Every one of the books which are so beautifully bound is a treasure.
   D. Regardless of consequences, he flew his plane toward the sound barrier.

28.____

29.
   A. To get the most out of country living, the surroundings must be peaceful.
   B. Had he heeded the warning, he would have saved himself much trouble.
   C. I can't understand his swimming beyond the safety zone.
   D. Take this book to the librarian.

29.____

30.
   A. Although he is playing golf only two years, he has already won three tournaments.
   B. The soil was so poor that despite the use of various fertilizers he was unable to effect an increase in the yield.
   C. None of the boys is better able to cope with the problem than he.
   D. He dived into the water; then he disappeared from sight.

30.____

31.
   A. Contrasted to his previous behavior, his actions today seemed almost saintly.
   B. If he would have reported on time, he would not have lost the job.
   C. His first answer, not his other answers, is open to question.
   D. He was much affected by the accident; the extent of his injuries is still to be determined.

31.____

32.
   A. He is one of those boys who always seem content.
   B. His excuse was different from the one I had expected.
   C. He may be more clever than me, but he doesn't work as hard.
   D. Walking along the road, he spied the girl's purse.

32.____

33.
   A. Of the two pictures which reached the final round of judging, I thought Gregg's was the better.
   B. The attitudes of children are often more carefree than their parents.
   C. Neither he nor I am to improve the situation.
   D. Every member of the group has submitted his report.

33.____

34. A. In the 70's and 80's there were many fewer luxuries than there are today.
    B. Among the contestants the best was obviously the youngest.
    C. This morning, at about eight o'clock, we saw an accident coming to school.
    D. I feel bad about his failure; nevertheless, he must adjust himself to the circumstances.

34.____

35. A. There were three obstacles to the project: the weather, the distance and the lack of proper equipment.
    B. He should have let us know whether he could come.
    C. Tom, Bill and Henry had a common fault-procrastination.
    D. If we wish to accomplish our purpose, we must cooperate together in the common cause.

35.____

36. A. The car has lain in the mud throughout the winter.
    B. Between you and me, this is a problem to be decided among all the delegates.
    C. After they had hung the noose from the beam, they hanged the outlaw.
    D. These kind of oranges do not have the pulpy center.

36.____

37. A. What the outcome was we shall never know.
    B. The interior can be completed by Monday night providing the materials arrive today.
    C. That's the unhappiest looking youngster in the school.
    D. Following the blast, he lay there helpless for hours.

37.____

38. A. Neither of the boys was willing to go.
    B. I am working, and always have, for the good of the organization.
    C. Before we left I hurried to his house to fetch him.
    D. Fearing that he would be late, he broke into a fast trot.

38.____

39. A. "I'll be there," she said, "even though my health is poor."
    B. "Have you seen the new picture, "The Wild Ones?"
    C. Mary and her sisters are sure to be there.
    D. The MONA LISA, which hangs in the Louvre, attracts throngs daily.

39.____

40. A. You will find the boy's equipment stored in the teacher's lounge.
    B. Walk three blocks north; then turn east one block.
    C. The new skyscraper is to be erected on Forty-ninth Street
    D. MACBETH was the one play he had read many, many times.

40.____

41. A. A carload of vegetables and fruits was destroyed by the flames.
    B. Neither Frank nor John is the correct choice for the job.
    C. The reason for the articles is because the paper is seeking a sensational issue.
    D. He was graduated from a local university, but not without great effort on his part.

41.____

42. A. Dinner being over, let us discuss the matter.
    B. It was no use continuing the effort, the door would not open.
    C. Drummond was born in the West, but the East was his home in later years.
    D. He would have liked to go.

42.____

43.　
A. If he had kept his mind on his work, he would not now be in such straits.
B. His graduation from High School was followed by a year of travel.
C. Everyone in the hall rose to his feet when the President entered.
D. They decided to reject whoever, by January 15, had not submitted his credentials.

43.____

44.　
A. Most of us teachers work hard.
B. Holding my hand up, I showed my approval.
C. The reason I take French is because I intend to travel.
D. Evidently it was not she whom we met.

44.____

45.　
A. Although glowing prospects of fabulous profits were pictured to him, he remained uninterested in the project.
B. Although the climate of Maine was much colder, he preferred it to California.
C. Although he protested his innocence, he could not escape the consequences of the mob's blind rage.
D. Although taciturn by nature, she chattered freely on her favorite subject, puppets.

45.____

46.　
A. Ladies' hats are more expensive now than ever.
B. They were frightened by his shrieking.
C. They were grateful to whomever would help them.
D. Large groups of persons visit the shrine daily.

46.____

47.　
A. On one side was a swamp, on the other a river.
B. Take those books next door.
C. John was running for our team when suddenly he drops the ball.
D. The data which were used had been supplied by the agents.

47.____

48.　
A. The constant droning of the bees caused me to drowse as I sat in the garden.
B. Swathed in bandages from head to foot, he was a pitiable sight.
C. We directed his attention to the girl who we believed most likely to be the prize winner.
D. There was little to choose among the many offerings.

48.____

49.　
A. Such consideration as you can give us will be appreciated.
B. It looks like another World War will break out any minute.
C. The boat sank at noon but it was early evening before the first rescuers arrived on the spot.
D. I had already eaten my lunch when the taxi arrived.

49.____

50.　
A. The girl whom I thought to be president was the secretary.
B. The truck which was here at three o'clock came for the chairs, not the refrigerator.
C. It is true that bright yellow apples are often lacking in firmness, but I enjoy those kind most.
D. Did you imply that he was competent?

50.____

KEY (CORRECT ANSWERS)

1. C	11. B	21. C	31. B	41. C
2. C	12. B	22. A	32. C	42. B
3. D	13. A	23. B	33. B	43. B
4. A	14. C	24. D	34. C	44. C
5. D	15. B	25. A	35. D	45. B
6. B	16. A	26. D	36. D	46. C
7. A	17. B	27. A	37. B	47. C
8. C	18. B	28. A	38. B	48. C
9. A	19. D	29. A	39. B	49. B
10. C	20. B	30. A	40. C	50. C

PREPARING WRITTEN MATERIAL
EXAMINATION SECTION
TEST 1

DIRECTIONS: Each question or incomplete statement is followed by several suggested answers or completions. Select the one that BEST answers the question or completes the statement. *PRINT THE LETTER OF THE CORRECT ANSWER IN THE SPACE AT THE RIGHT.*

Questions 1-4.

DIRECTIONS: Questions 1 through 4 each consist of a sentence which may or may not be an example of good English. The underlined parts of each sentence may be correct or incorrect. Examine each sentence, considering grammar, punctuation, spelling, and capitalization. If the English usage in the underlined parts of the sentence given is better than any of the changes in the underlined words suggested in options B, C, or D, choose option A. If the changes in the underlined words suggested in options B, C, or D would make the sentence correct, choose the correct option. Do not choose an option that will change the meaning of the sentence.

1. This <u>Fall</u>, the office will be closed on <u>Columbus Day</u>, <u>October</u> 9th. 1.____
   A. Correct as is
   B. fall…Columbus Day; October
   C. Fall…columbus day, October
   D. fall…Columbus Day – October

2. There <u>weren't no</u> paper in the supply closet. 2.____
   A. Correct as is
   B. weren't any
   C. wasn't any
   D. wasn't no

3. The <u>alphabet, or A to Z sequence are</u> the basis of most filing systems. 3.____
   A. Correct as is
   B. alphabet, or A to Z sequence, is
   C. alphabet, or A to Z sequence, are
   D. alphabet, or A too Z sequence, is

4. The Office Aide checked the <u>register and finding</u> the date of the meeting. 4.____
   A. Correct as is
   B. regaster and finding
   C. register and found
   D. regaster and found

Questions 5-10.

DIRECTIONS: Questions 5 through 10 consist of sentences which contain examples of correct or incorrect English usage. Examine each sentence with reference to grammar, spelling, punctuation, and capitalization. Chooses one of the following options that would be BEST for correct English usage:

133

2 (#1)

  A. The sentence is correct
  B. There is one mistake
  C. There are two mistakes
  D. There are three mistakes

5. Mrs. Fitzgerald came to the 59th Precinct to retreive her property which were stolen earlier in the week. 5.____

6. The two officer's responded to the call, only to find that the perpatrator and the victim have left the scene. 6.____

7. Mr. Coleman called the 61st Precinct to report that, upon arriving at his store, he discovered that there was a large hole in the wall and that three boxes of radios were missing. 7.____

8. The Administrative Leiutenant of the 62nd Precinct held a meeting which was attended by all the civilians, assigned to the Precinct. 8.____

9. Three days after the robbery occurred the detective apprahended two suspects and recovered the stolen items. 9.____

10. The Community Affairs Officer of the 64th Precinct is the liaison between the Precinct and the community; he works closely with various community organizations, and elected officials, 10.____

Questions 11-18.

DIRECTIONS: Questions 11 through 18 are to be answered on the basis of the following paragraph, which contains some deliberate errors in spelling and/or grammar and/or punctuation. Each line of the paragraph is preceded by a number. There are 9 lines and 9 numbers.

Line No.	Paragraph Line
1	The protection of life and proporty are, one of
2	the oldest and most important functions of a city.
3	New York City has it's own full-time police Agency.
4	The police Department has the power an it shall
5	be there duty to preserve the Public piece,
6	prevent crime detect and arrest offenders, supress
7	riots, protect the rites of persons and property, etc.
8	The maintainance of sound relations with the community they
9	serve is an important function of law enforcement officers

11. How many errors are contained in line one? 11.____

12. How many errors are contained in line two? 12.____

13. How many errors are contained in line three? 13.____

14. How many errors are contained in line four? 14._____

15. How many errors are contained in line five? 15._____

16. How many errors are contained in line six? 16._____

17. How many errors are contained in line seven? 17._____

18. How many errors are contained in line eight? 18._____

19. In the sentence, *The candidate wants to file his application for preference before it is too late*, the word *before* is used as a(n) 19._____
    A. preposition
    B. subordinating conjunction
    C. pronoun
    D. adverb

20. The one of the following sentences which is grammatically PREFERABLE to the others is: 20._____
    A. Our engineers will go over your blueprints so that you may have no problems in construction.
    B. For a long time he had been arguing that we, not he, are to blame for the confusion.
    C. I worked on this automobile for two hours and still cannot find out what is wrong with it.
    D. Accustomed to all kinds of hardships, fatigue seldom bothers veteran policemen.

KEY (CORRECT ANSWERS)

1.	A	11.	C
2.	C	12.	D
3.	B	13.	C
4.	C	14.	B
5.	C	15.	C
6.	D	16.	B
7.	A	17.	A
8.	C	18.	A
9.	C	19.	B
10.	B	20.	A

TEST 2

DIRECTIONS: Each question or incomplete statement is followed by several suggested answers or completions. Select the one that BEST answers the question or completes the statement. *PRINT THE LETTER OF THE CORRECT ANSWER IN THE SPACE AT THE RIGHT.*

1. The plural of
   A. turkey is turkies
   B. cargo is cargoes
   C. bankruptcy is bankruptcys
   D. son-in-law is son-in-laws

   1.____

2. The abbreviation *viz.* means MOST NEARLY
   A. namely   B. for example   C. the following   D. see

   2.____

3. In the sentence, *A man in a light-grey suit waited thirty-five minutes in the ante-room for the all-important document,* the word IMPROPERLY hyphenated is
   A. light-grey   B. thirty-five   C. ante-room   D. all-important

   3.____

4. The MOST accurate of the following sentences is:
   A. The commissioner, as well as his deputy and various bureau heads, were present.
   B. A new organization of employers and employees have been formed.
   C. One or the other of these men have been selected.
   D. The number of pages in the book is enough to discourage a reader.

   4.____

5. The MOST accurate of the following sentences is:
   A. Between you and me, I think he is the better man.
   B. He was believed to be me.
   C. Is it us that you wish to see?
   D. The winners are him and her.

   5.____

Questions 6-13.

DIRECTIONS: The sentences numbered 6 through 13 deal with some phase of police activity. They may be classified most appropriately under one of the following four categories.

   A. Faulty because of incorrect grammar
   B. Faulty because of incorrect punctuation
   C. Faulty because of incorrect use of a word
   D. Correct

Examine each sentence carefully. Then, in the space at the right, print the capital letter preceding the option which is the BEST of the four suggested above. All incorrect sentences contain only one type of error. Consider a sentence correct if it contains none of the types of errors mentioned, even though there may be other correct ways of expressing the same thought.

6. The Department Medal of Honor is awarded to a member of the Police Force who distinguishes himself inconspicuously in the line of police duty by the performance of an act of gallantry.

6.____

7. Members of the Detective Division are charged with the prevention of crime, the detection and arrest of criminals and the recovery of lost or stolen property,

7.____

8. Detectives are selected from the uniformed patrol forces after they have indicated by conduct, aptitude and performance that they are qualified for the more intricate duties of a detective.

8.____

9. The patrolman, pursuing his assailant, exchanged shots with the gunman and immortally wounded him as he fled into a nearby building.

9.____

10. The members of the Traffic Division has to enforce the Vehicle and Traffic Law, the Traffic Regulations and ordinances relating to vehicular and pedestrian traffic.

10.____

11. After firing a shot at the gunman, the crowd dispersed from the patrolman's line of fire.

11.____

12. The efficiency of the Missing Persons Bureau is maintained with a maximum of public personnel due to the specialized training given to its members.

12.____

13. Records of persons arrested for violations of Vehicle and Traffic Regulations are transmitted upon request to precincts, courts and other authorized agencies.

13.____

14. Following are two sentences which may or may not be written in correct English:
    I. Two clients assaulted the officer.
    II. The van is illegally parked.
   Which one of the following statements is CORRECT?
   A. Only Sentence I is written in correct English.
   B. Only Sentence II is written in correct English.
   C. Sentences I and II are both written in correct English.
   D. Neither Sentence I nor Sentence II is written in correct English.

14.____

15. Following are two sentences which may or may not be written in correct English:
    I. Security Officer Rollo escorted the visitor to the patrolroom.
    II. Two entry were made in the facility logbook.
   Which one of the following statements is CORRECT?
   A. Only Sentence I is written in correct English.
   B. Only Sentence II is written in correct English.
   C. Sentences I and II are both written in correct English.
   D. Neither Sentence I nor Sentence II is written in correct English.

15.____

16. Following are two sentences which may or may not be written in correct English:
    I. Officer McElroy putted out a small fire in the wastepaper basket.
    II. Special Officer Janssen told the visitor where he could obtained a pass.
    Which one of the following statements is CORRECT?
    A. Only Sentence I is written in correct English.
    B. Only Sentence II is written in correct English.
    C. Sentences I and II are both written in correct English.
    D. Neither Sentence I nor Sentence II is written in correct English.

16._____

17. Following are two sentences which may or may not be written in correct English:
    I. Security Officer Warren observed a broken window while he was on his post in Hallway C.
    II. The worker reported that two typewriters had been stolen from the office,
    Which one of the following statements is CORRECT?
    A. Only Sentence I is written in correct English.
    B. Only Sentence II is written in correct English.
    C. Sentences I and II are both written in correct English.
    D. Neither Sentence I nor Sentence II is written in correct English,

17._____

18. Following are two sentences which may or may not be written in correct English:
    I. Special Officer Cleveland was attempting to calm an emotionally disturbed visitor.
    II. The visitor did not stop crying and calling for his wife.
    Which one of the following statements is CORRECT?
    A. Only Sentence I is written in correct English.
    B. Only Sentence II is written in correct English.
    C. Sentences I and II are both written in correct English.
    D. Neither Sentence I nor Sentence II is written in correct English.

18._____

19. Following are two sentences that may or may not be written in correct English:
    I. While on patrol, I observes a vagrant loitering near the drug dispensary.
    II. I escorted the vagrant out of the building and off the premises.
    Which one of the following statements is CORRECT?
    A. Only Sentence I is written in correct English.
    B. Only Sentence II is written in correct English.
    C. Sentences I and II are both written in correct English.
    D. Neither Sentence I nor Sentence II is written in correct English.

19._____

20. Following are two sentences which may or may not be written in correct English:
    I. At 4:00 P.M., Sergeant Raymond told me to evacuate the waiting area immediately due to a bomb threat.
    II. Some of the clients did not want to leave the building.
    Which one of the following statements is CORRECT?
    A. Only Sentence I is written in correct English.
    B. Only Sentence II is written in correct English.
    C. Sentences I and II are both written in correct English.
    D. Neither Sentence I nor Sentence II is written in correct English.

20._____

KEY (CORRECT ANSWERS)

1.	B	11.	A
2.	A	12.	C
3.	C	13.	D
4.	D	14.	C
5.	A	15.	A
6.	C	16.	D
7.	B	17.	A
8.	D	18.	A
9.	C	19.	B
10.	A	20.	C

PREPARING WRITTEN MATERIAL

PARAGRAPH REARRANGEMENT
COMMENTARY

The sentences that follow are in scrambled order. You are to rearrange them in proper order and indicate the letter choice containing the correct answer at the space at the right.

Each group of sentences in this section is actually a paragraph presented in scrambled order. Each sentence in the group has a place in that paragraph; no sentence is to be left out. You are to read each group of sentences and decide upon the best order in which to put the sentences so as to form a well-organized paragraph.

The questions in this section measure the ability to solve a problem when all the facts relevant to its solution are not given.

More specifically, certain positions of responsibility and authority require the employee to discover connection between events sometimes, apparently, unrelated. In order to do this, the employee will find it necessary to correctly infer that unspecified events have probably occurred or are likely to occur. This ability becomes especially important when action must be taken on incomplete information.

Accordingly, these questions require competitors to choose among several suggested alternatives, each of which presents a different sequential arrangement of the events. Competitors must choose the MOST logical of the suggested sequences.

In order to do so, they may be required to draw on general knowledge to infer missing concepts or events that are essential to sequencing the given events. Competitors should be careful to infer only what is essential to the sequence. The plausibility of the wrong alternatives will always require the inclusion of unlikely events or of additional chains of events which are NOT essential to sequencing the given events.

It's very important to remember that you are looking for the best of the four possible choices, and that the best choice of all may not even be one of the answers you're given to choose from.

There is no one right way to solve these problems. Many people have found it helpful to first write out the order of the sentences, as they would have arranged them, on their scrap paper before looking at the possible answers. If their optimum answer is there, this can save them some time. If it isn't, this method can still give insight into solving the problem. Others find it most helpful to just go through each of the possible choices, contrasting each as they go along. You should use whatever method feels comfortable and works for you.

While most of these types of questions are not that difficult, we've added a higher percentage of the difficult type, just to give you more practice. Usually there are only one or two questions on this section that contain such subtle distinctions that you're unable to answer confidently. And you then may find yourself stuck deciding between two possible choices, neither of which you're sure about.

EXAMINATION SECTION
TEST 1

DIRECTIONS: Each question consists of several sentences which can be arranged in a logical sequence. For each question, select the choice which places the numbered sentences in the MOST logical sequence. *PRINT THE LETTER OF THE CORRECT ANSWER IN THE SPACE AT THE RIGHT.*

1.
   I. A body was found in the woods.
   II. A man proclaimed innocence.
   III. The owner of a gun was located.
   IV. A gun was traced.
   V. The owner of a gun was questioned.
   The CORRECT answer is:
   A. IV, III, V, II, I   B. II, I, IV, III, V   C. I, IV, III, V, II
   D. I, III, V, II, IV   E. I, II, IV, III, V

   1.____

2.
   I. A man is in a hunting accident.
   II. A man fell down a flight of steps.
   III. A man lost his vision in one eye,
   IV. A man broke his leg.
   V. A man had to walk with a cane.
   The CORRECT answer is:
   A. II, IV, V, I, III   B. IV, V, I, III, II   C. III, I, IV, V, II
   D. I, III, V, II, IV   E. I, III, II, IV, V

   2.____

3.
   I. A man is offered a new job.
   II. A woman is offered a new job.
   III. A man works as a waiter.
   IV. A woman works as a waitress.
   V. A woman gives notice.
   The CORRECT answer is:
   A. IV, II, V, III, I   B. IV, II, V, I, III   C. II, IV, V, III, I
   D. III, I, IV, II, V   E. IV, III, II, V, I

   3.____

4.
   I. A train let the station late.
   II. A man was late for work.
   III. A man lost his job.
   IV. Many people complained because the train was late.
   V. There was a traffic jam.
   The CORRECT answer is:
   A. V, II, I, IV, III   B. V, I, IV, II, III   C. V, I, II, IV, III
   D. I, V, IV, II, III   E. II, I, IV, V, III

   4.____

143

5.
I. The burden of proof as to each issue is determined before trial and remains upon the same party throughout the trial.
II. The jury is at liberty to believe one witness' testimony as against a number of contradictory witnesses.
III. In a civil case, the party bearing the burden of proof is required to prove his contention by a fair preponderance of the evidence.
IV. However, it must be noted that a fair preponderance of evidence does not necessarily mean a greater number of witnesses.
V. The burden of proof is the burden which rests upon one of the parties to an action to persuade the trier of the facts, generally the jury, that a proposition he asserts is true.
VI. If the evidence is equally balanced, or if it leaves the jury in such doubt as to be unable to decide the controversy either way, judgment must be given against the party upon whom the burden of proof rests.

The CORRECT answer is:
A. III, II, V, IV, I, VI   B. I, II, VI, V, III, IV   C. III, IV, V, I, II, VI
D. V, I, III, VI, IV, II   E. I, V, III, VI, IV, II

6.
I. If a parent is without assets and is unemployed, he cannot be convicted of the crime of non-support of a child.
II. The term *sufficient ability* has been held to mean sufficient financial ability.
III. It does not matter if his unemployment is by choice or unavoidable circumstances.
IV. If he fails to take any steps at all, he may be liable to prosecution for endangering the welfare of a child.
V. Under the penal law, a parent is responsible for the support of his minor child only if the parent is of *sufficient ability*.
VI. An indigent parent may meet his obligation by borrowing money or by seeking aid under the provisions of the Social Welfare Law.

The CORRECT answer is:
A. VI, I, V, III, II, IV   B. I, III, V, II, IV, VI   C. V, II, I, III, VI, IV
D. I, VI, IV, V, II, III   E. II, V, I, III, VI, IV

7.
I. Consider, for example, the case of a rabble rouser who urges a group of twenty people to go out and break the windows of a nearby factory.
II. Therefore, the law fills the indicated gap with the crime of *inciting to riot.*
III. A person is considered guilty of inciting to riot when he urges ten or more persons to engage in tumultuous and violent conduct of a kind likely to create public alarm.
IV. However, if he has not obtained the cooperation of at least four people, he cannot be charged with unlawful assembly.
V. The charge of inciting to riot was added to the law to cover types of conduct which cannot be classified as either the crime of *riot* or the crime of *unlawful assembly*.
VI. If he acquires the acquiescence of at least four of them, he is guilty of unlawful assembly even if the project does not materialize.

The CORRECT answer is:
A. III, V, I, VI, IV, II   B. V, I, IV, VI, II, III   C. III, IV, I, V, II, VI
D. V, I, IV, VI, III, II   E. V, III, I, VI, IV, II

8. I. If, however, the rebuttal evidence presents an issue of credibility, it is for the jury to determine whether the presumption has, in fact, been destroyed.
    II. Once sufficient evidence to the contrary is introduced, the presumption disappears from the trial.
    III. The effect of a presumption is to place the burden upon the adversary to come forward with evidence to rebut the presumption.
    IV. When a presumption is overcome and ceases to exist in the case, the fact or facts which gave rise to the presumption still remain.
    V. Whether a presumption has been overcome is ordinarily a question for the court.
    VI. Such information may furnish a basis for a logical inference.
    The CORRECT answer is:
    A. IV, VI, II, V, I, III   B. III, II, V, I, IV, VI   C. V, III, VI, IV, II, I
    D. V, IV, I, II, VI, III   E. II, III, V, I, IV, VI

8.____

9. I. An executive may answer a letter by writing his reply on the face of the letter itself instead of having a return letter typed.
    II. This procedure is efficient because it saves the executive's time, the typist's time, and saves office file space.
    III. Copying machines are used in small offices as well as large offices to save time and money in making brief replies to business letters.
    IV. A copy is made on a copying machine to go into the company files, while the original is mailed back to the sender.
    The CORRECT answer is:
    A. I, II, IV, III   B. I, IV, II, III   C. III, I, IV, II   D. III, IV, II, I

9.____

10. I. Most organizations favor one of the types but always include the others to a lesser degree.
    II. However, we can detect a definite trend toward greater use of symbolic control.
    III. We suggest that our local police agencies are today primarily utilizing material control.
    IV. Control can be classified into three types: physical, material, and symbolic.
    The CORRECT answer is:
    A. IV, II, III, I   B. II, I, IV, III   C. III, IV, II, I   D. IV, I, III, II

10.____

11. I. Project residents had first claim to this use, followed by surrounding neighborhood children.
    II. By contrast, recreation space within the project's interior was found to be used more often by both groups.
    III. Studies of the use of project grounds in many cities showed grounds left open for public use were neglected and unused, both by residents and by members of the surrounding community.
    IV. Project residents had clearly laid claim to the play spaces, setting up and enforcing unwritten rules for use.
    V. Each group, by experience, found their activities easily disrupted by other groups, and their claim to the use of space for recreation difficult to enforce.

11.____

The CORRECT answer is:
A. IV, V, I, II, III
B. V, II, IV, III, I
C. I, IV, III, II, V
D. III, V, II, IV, I

12. I. They do not consider the problems correctable within the existing subsidy formula and social policy of accepting all eligible applicants regardless of social behavior.
    II. A recent survey, however, indicated that tenants believe these problems correctable by local housing authorities and management within the existing financial formula.
    III. Many of the problems and complaints concerning public housing management and design have created resentment between the tenant and the landlord.
    IV. This same survey indicated that administrators and managers do not agree with the tenants.
    The CORRECT answer is:
    A. II, I, III, IV B. I, III, IV, II C. III, II, IV, I D. IV, II, I, III

12.____

13. I. In single-family residences, there is usually enough distance between tenants to prevent occupants from annoying one another.
    II. For example, a certain small percentage of tenant families has one or more members addicted to alcohol.
    III. While managers believe in the right of individuals to live as they choose, the manager becomes concerned when the pattern of living jeopardizes others' rights.
    IV. Still others turn night into day, staging lusty entertainments which carry on into the hours when most tenants are trying to sleep.
    V. In apartment buildings, however, tenants live so closely together that any misbehavior can result in unpleasant living conditions.
    VI. Other families engage in violent argument.
    The CORRECT answer is:
    A. III, II, V, IV, VI, I
    B. I, V, II, VI, IV, III
    C. II, V, IV, I, III, VI
    D. IV, II, V, VI, III, I

13.____

14. I. Congress made the commitment explicit in the Housing Act of 194, establishing as a national goal the realization of a *decent home and suitable environment for every American family*.
    II. The result has been that the goal of decent home and suitable environment is still as far distant as ever for the disadvantaged urban family.
    III. In spite of this action by Congress, federal housing programs have continued to be fragmented and grossly underfunded.
    IV. The passage of the National Housing Act signaled a few federal commitment to provide housing for the nation's citizens.
    The CORRECT answer is:
    A. I, IV, III, II B. IV, I, III, II C. IV, I, II, III D. II, IV, I, III

14.____

15.
I. The greater expense does not necessarily involve *exploitation*, but it is often perceived as exploitative and unfair by those who are aware of the price differences involved, but unaware of operating costs.
II. Ghetto residents believe they are *exploited* by local merchants, and evidence substantiates some of these beliefs.
III. However, stores in low-income areas were more likely to be small independents, which could not achieve the economies available to supermarket chains and were, therefore, more likely to charge higher prices, and the customers were more likely to buy smaller-sized packages which are more expensive per unit of measure.
IV. A study conducted in one city showed that distinctly higher prices were charged for goods sold in ghetto stores in other areas.
The CORRECT answer is:
  A. IV, II, I, III   B. IV, I, III, II   C. II, IV, III, I   D. II, III, IV, I

15._____

KEY (CORRECT ANSWERS)

1.	C	6.	C	11.	D
2.	E	7.	A	12.	C
3.	B	8.	B	13.	B
4.	B	9.	C	14.	B
5.	D	10.	D	15.	C

COURTROOM TERMS

A/K/A: Acronym that stands for "also known as" and introduces any alternative or assumed names or aliases of an individual. A term to indicate another name by which a person is known.

Arraignment: The bringing of a defendant before the court to answer the matters charged against him in an indictment or information. The defendant is read the charges and must respond with his plea.

Arrest: Deprivation of one's liberty by legal authority.

Bail: An amount of money set by the court to procure the release of a person from legal custody; this money is to be forfeited if the defendant fails to appear for trial.

Beyond a Reasonable Doubt: The standard of proof required for a finding of guilty in a criminal matter. Satisfied to a moral certainty. This is a higher standard of proof than that required in a civil matter (preponderance of the evidence).

Co-Defendant: Any additional defendant or respondent in the same case.

Confession: A voluntary statement made by a person charged with a crime wherein said person acknowledges his/her guilt of the offense charged and discloses participation in the act.

Controlled Dangerous Substance: That group of legally designated drugs, which, by statute, it is illegal to possess or distribute.

Criminal complaint: The initial written notice to a defendant that he/she is being charged with a public offense.

Due Process of Law: The exercise of the powers of the government with the safeguards for the protection of individual rights as set forth in the constitution, statutes, and common case law.

Felony: A crime of a more serious nature than a misdemeanor, the exact nature of which is defined by state statute and which is punishable by a term of imprisonment exceeding one year or by death.

Grand Jury: A jury of inquiry whose duty is to receive complaints and accusations in criminal cases, hear the evidence presented on the part of the state, and determine whether to indict (see "indictment" below).

Impeach: As used in the Law of Evidence, to call into question the truthfulness of a witness, by means of introducing evidence to discredit him or her.

Indictment: A written accusation presented by a grand jury after having been presented with evidence, charging that a person named therein has done some act, or has been guilty of some omission that by law is a public offense.

Miranda Warnings: The compulsory advisement of a person's rights prior to any custodial interrogation; these include: a) the right to remain silent; b) that any statement made may be used against him/her; c) the right to an attorney; d) the appointment of counsel if the accused cannot afford his or her own attorney. Unless these rights are given, any evidence obtained in an interrogation cannot be used in the individual's trial against him/her.

Misdemeanor: Offense lower than felony and generally punishable by a fine or imprisonment other than in a penitentiary.

Motion to Quash: Application to the court to set aside the complaint, indictment or subpoena due to a lack of probable cause to arrest the defendant, or in matters heard by a grand jury, due to evidence not properly presented to the grand jury.

Motion to Sever: Application to the court made when there are two defendants charged with the same crimes or who acted jointly in the commission of a crime, when their attorneys feel it would be in their best interest if they had separate trials.

Motion to Suppress Evidence: Application to the court to prevent evidence from being presented at trial when said evidence has been obtained by illegal means. It applies to physical evidence, statements made by defendant when not advised by counsel or through wiretapping, prior convictions, etc..

Parole: A conditional release from custody at the discretion of the paroling authority prior to his or her completing the prison sentence imposed. During said release the offender is required to observe conditions of this status under the supervision of a parole agency.

Plea: A defendant's formal answer in court to the charges contained in a charging document.

Guilty: A plea by the defendant in which he acknowledges guilt either of the offense charged or of a less serious offense pursuant to an agreement with the prosecuting attorney. It should be understood, however, that the court may not be obliged to recognize this.

Nolo Contendere: A plea that is admissible in some jurisdictions, in which the defendant states that he does not contest the charges against him. Also called "no contest", this plea has the same effect as a guilty plea, except that it cannot be used against the defendant in civil actions arising out of the same incident which gave rise to the criminal charges.

Not Guilty: A plea of innocence by the defendant.

Not Guilty by Reason of Insanity: A plea that is sometimes entered in conjunction with the "not guilty" plea.

Double Jeopardy: A plea entered by a defendant who has been tried for an offense wherein he asserts that he cannot be tried a second time for said offense, unless he successfully secured a new trial after an appeal, or after a motion for a new trial was granted by the trial court.

Police Report: The official report made by any police officer involved with the incident or appearing after the incident, setting forth the officer's observations and statements of parties and witnesses. It can be used as evidence in a trial.

Pre-Trial Intervention: Utilized in some states when a defendant is accused of a first offense, to divert the defendant from the criminal justice system.

Probation: To allow a person convicted of a minor offense to go at large, under a suspension of sentence, during good behavior, and generally under the supervision of a probation officer.

Prosecutor: The attorney who prosecutes defendants for crimes, in the name of the government.

Search Warrant: A written order, issued by the court, directing the police to search a specified location for particular personal property (stolen or illegally possessed).

Speedy Trial: Mandate by the government that all criminal trials must take place within a specified time after arrest.

Writ of Habeas Corpus: A mandate issued from a court requiring that an individual be brought before the court.

GLOSSARY OF LEGAL TERMS

TABLE OF CONTENTS

	Page
Action ... Affiant	1
Affidavit ... At Bar	2
At Issue ... Burden of Proof	3
Business ... Commute	4
Complainant ... Conviction	5
Cooperative ... Demur (v.)	6
Demurrage ... Endorsement	7
Enjoin ... Facsimile	8
Factor ... Guilty	9
Habeas Corpus ... Incumbrance	10
Indemnify ... Laches	11
Landlord and Tenant ... Malice	12
Mandamus ... Obiter Dictum	13
Object (v.) ... Perjury	14
Perpetuity ... Proclamation	15
Proffered Evidence ... Referee	16
Referendum ... Stare Decisis	17
State ... Term	18
Testamentary ... Warrant (Warranty) (v.)	19
Warrant (n.) ... Zoning	20

GLOSSARY OF LEGAL TERMS

A

ACTION - "Action" includes a civil action and a criminal action.
A FORTIORI - A term meaning you can reason one thing from the existence of certain facts.
A POSTERIORI - From what goes after; from effect to cause.
A PRIORI - From what goes before; from cause to effect.
AB INITIO - From the beginning.
ABATE - To diminish or put an end to.
ABET - To encourage the commission of a crime.
ABEYANCE - Suspension, temporary suppression.
ABIDE - To accept the consequences of.
ABJURE - To renounce; give up.
ABRIDGE - To reduce; contract; diminish.
ABROGATE - To annul, repeal, or destroy.
ABSCOND - To hide or absent oneself to avoid legal action.
ABSTRACT - A summary.
ABUT - To border on, to touch.
ACCESS - Approach; in real property law it means the right of the owner of property to the use of the highway or road next to his land, without obstruction by intervening property owners.
ACCESSORY - In criminal law, it means the person who contributes or aids in the commission of a crime.
ACCOMMODATED PARTY - One to whom credit is extended on the strength of another person signing a commercial paper.
ACCOMMODATION PAPER - A commercial paper to which the accommodating party has put his name.
ACCOMPLICE - In criminal law, it means a person who together with the principal offender commits a crime.
ACCORD - An agreement to accept something different or less than that to which one is entitled, which extinguishes the entire obligation.
ACCOUNT - A statement of mutual demands in the nature of debt and credit between parties.
ACCRETION - The act of adding to a thing; in real property law, it means gradual accumulation of land by natural causes.
ACCRUE - To grow to; to be added to.
ACKNOWLEDGMENT - The act of going before an official authorized to take acknowledgments, and acknowledging an act as one's own.
ACQUIESCENCE - A silent appearance of consent.
ACQUIT - To legally determine the innocence of one charged with a crime.
AD INFINITUM - Indefinitely.
AD LITEM - For the suit.
AD VALOREM - According to value.
ADJECTIVE LAW - Rules of procedure.
ADJUDICATION - The judgment given in a case.
ADMIRALTY - Court having jurisdiction over maritime cases.
ADULT - Sixteen years old or over (in criminal law).
ADVANCE - In commercial law, it means to pay money or render other value before it is due.
ADVERSE - Opposed; contrary.
ADVOCATE - (v.) To speak in favor of;
(n.) One who assists, defends, or pleads for another.
AFFIANT - A person who makes and signs an affidavit.

AFFIDAVIT - A written and sworn to declaration of facts, voluntarily made.
AFFINITY - The relationship between persons through marriage with the kindred of each other; distinguished from consanguinity, which is the relationship by blood.
AFFIRM - To ratify; also when an appellate court affirms a judgment, decree, or order, it means that it is valid and right and must stand as rendered in the lower court.
AFOREMENTIONED; AFORESAID - Before or already said.
AGENT - One who represents and acts for another.
AID AND COMFORT - To help; encourage.
ALIAS - A name not one's true name.
ALIBI - A claim of not being present at a certain place at a certain time.
ALLEGE - To assert.
ALLOTMENT - A share or portion.
AMBIGUITY - Uncertainty; capable of being understood in more than one way.
AMENDMENT - Any language made or proposed as a change in some principal writing.
AMICUS CURIAE - A friend of the court; one who has an interest in a case, although not a party in the case, who volunteers advice upon matters of law to the judge. For example, a brief amicus curiae.
AMORTIZATION - To provide for a gradual extinction of (a future obligation) in advance of maturity, especially, by periodical contributions to a sinking fund which will be adequate to discharge a debt or make a replacement when it becomes necessary.
ANCILLARY - Aiding, auxiliary.
ANNOTATION - A note added by way of comment or explanation.
ANSWER - A written statement made by a defendant setting forth the grounds of his defense.
ANTE - Before.
ANTE MORTEM - Before death.
APPEAL - The removal of a case from a lower court to one of superior jurisdiction for the purpose of obtaining a review.
APPEARANCE - Coming into court as a party to a suit.
APPELLANT - The party who takes an appeal from one court or jurisdiction to another (appellate) court for review.
APPELLEE - The party against whom an appeal is taken.
APPROPRIATE - To make a thing one's own.
APPROPRIATION - Prescribing the destination of a thing; the act of the legislature designating a particular fund, to be applied to some object of government expenditure.
APPURTENANT - Belonging to; accessory or incident to.
ARBITER - One who decides a dispute; a referee.
ARBITRARY - Unreasoned; not governed by any fixed rules or standard.
ARGUENDO - By way of argument.
ARRAIGN - To call the prisoner before the court to answer to a charge.
ASSENT - A declaration of willingness to do something in compliance with a request.
ASSERT - Declare.
ASSESS - To fix the rate or amount.
ASSIGN - To transfer; to appoint; to select for a particular purpose.
ASSIGNEE - One who receives an assignment.
ASSIGNOR - One who makes an assignment.
AT BAR - Before the court.

AT ISSUE - When parties in an action come to a point where one asserts something and the other denies it.
ATTACH - Seize property by court order and sometimes arrest a person.
ATTEST - To witness a will, etc.; act of attestation.
AVERMENT - A positive statement of facts.

B

BAIL - To obtain the release of a person from legal custody by giving security and promising that he shall appear in court; to deliver (goods, etc.) in trust to a person for a special purpose.
BAILEE - One to whom personal property is delivered under a contract of bailment.
BAILMENT - Delivery of personal property to another to be held for a certain purpose and to be returned when the purpose is accomplished.
BAILOR - The party who delivers goods to another, under a contract of bailment.
BANC (OR BANK) - Bench; the place where a court sits permanently or regularly; also the assembly of all the judges of a court.
BANKRUPT - An insolvent person, technically, one declared to be bankrupt after a bankruptcy proceeding.
BAR - The legal profession.
BARRATRY - Exciting groundless judicial proceedings.
BARTER - A contract by which parties exchange goods for other goods.
BATTERY - Illegal interfering with another's person.
BEARER - In commercial law, it means the person in possession of a commercial paper which is payable to the bearer.
BENCH - The court itself or the judge.
BENEFICIARY - A person benefiting under a will, trust, or agreement.
BEST EVIDENCE RULE,THE - Except as otherwise provided by statute, no evidence other than the writing itself is admissible to prove the content of a writing. This section shall be known and may be cited as the best evidence rule.
BEQUEST - A gift of personal property under a will.
BILL - A formal written statement of complaint to a court of justice; also, a draft of an act of the legislature before it becomes a law; also, accounts for goods sold, services rendered, or work done.
BONA FIDE - In or with good faith; honestly.
BOND - An instrument by which the maker promises to pay a sum of money to another, usually providing that upon performances of a certain condition the obligation shall be void.
BOYCOTT - A plan to prevent the carrying on of a business by wrongful means.
BREACH - The breaking or violating of a law, or the failure to carry out a duty.
BRIEF - A written document, prepared by a lawyer to serve as the basis of an argument upon a case in court, usually an appellate court.
BURDEN OF PRODUCING EVIDENCE - The obligation of a party to introduce evidence sufficient to avoid a ruling against him on the issue.
BURDEN OF PROOF - The obligation of a party to establish by evidence a requisite degree of belief concerning a fact in the mind of the trier of fact or the court. The burden of proof may require a party to raise a reasonable doubt concerning the existence of nonexistence of a fact or that he establish the existence or nonexistence of a fact by a preponderance of the evidence, by clear and convincing proof, or by proof beyond a reasonable doubt.

Except as otherwise provided by law, the burden of proof requires proof by a preponderance of the evidence.

BUSINESS, A - Shall include every kind of business, profession, occupation, calling or operation of institutions, whether carried on for profit or not.

BY-LAWS - Regulations, ordinances, or rules enacted by a corporation, association, etc., for its own government.

C

CANON - A doctrine; also, a law or rule, of a church or association in particular.

CAPIAS - An order to arrest.

CAPTION - In a pleading, deposition or other paper connected with a case in court, it is the heading or introductory clause which shows the names of the parties, name of the court, number of the case on the docket or calendar, etc.

CARRIER - A person or corporation undertaking to transport persons or property.

CASE - A general term for an action, cause, suit, or controversy before a judicial body.

CAUSE - A suit, litigation or action before a court.

CAVEAT EMPTOR - Let the buyer beware. This term expresses the rule that the purchaser of an article must examine, judge, and test it for himself, being bound to discover any obvious defects or imperfections.

CERTIFICATE - A written representation that some legal formality has been complied with.

CERTIORARI - To be informed of; the name of a writ issued by a superior court directing the lower court to send up to the former the record and proceedings of a case.

CHANGE OF VENUE - To remove place of trial from one place to another.

CHARGE - An obligation or duty; a formal complaint; an instruction of the court to the jury upon a case.

CHARTER - (n.) The authority by virtue of which an organized body acts;
(v.) in mercantile law, it means to hire or lease a vehicle or vessel for transportation.

CHATTEL - An article of personal property.

CHATTEL MORTGAGE - A mortgage on personal property.

CIRCUIT - A division of the country, for the administration of justice; a geographical area served by a court.

CITATION - The act of the court by which a person is summoned or cited; also, a reference to legal authority.

CIVIL (ACTIONS)- It indicates the private rights and remedies of individuals in contrast to the word "criminal" (actions) which relates to prosecution for violation of laws.

CLAIM (n.) - Any demand held or asserted as of right.

CODICIL - An addition to a will.

CODIFY - To arrange the laws of a country into a code.

COGNIZANCE - Notice or knowledge.

COLLATERAL - By the side; accompanying; an article or thing given to secure performance of a promise.

COMITY - Courtesy; the practice by which one court follows the decision of another court on the same question.

COMMIT - To perform, as an act; to perpetrate, as a crime; to send a person to prison.

COMMON LAW - As distinguished from law created by the enactment of the legislature (called statutory law), it relates to those principles and rules of action which derive their authority solely from usages and customs of immemorial antiquity, particularly with reference to the ancient unwritten law of England. The written pronouncements of the common law are found in court decisions.

COMMUTE - Change punishment to one less severe.

COMPLAINANT - One who applies to the court for legal redress.
COMPLAINT - The pleading of a plaintiff in a civil action; or a charge that a person has committed a specified offense.
COMPROMISE - An arrangement for settling a dispute by agreement.
CONCUR - To agree, consent.
CONCURRENT - Running together, at the same time.
CONDEMNATION - Taking private property for public use on payment therefor.
CONDITION - Mode or state of being; a qualification or restriction.
CONDUCT - Active and passive behavior; both verbal and nonverbal.
CONFESSION - Voluntary statement of guilt of crime.
CONFIDENTIAL COMMUNICATION BETWEEN CLIENT AND LAWYER - Information transmitted between a client and his lawyer in the course of that relationship and in confidence by a means which, so far as the client is aware, discloses the information to no third persons other than those who are present to further the interest of the client in the consultation or those to whom disclosure is reasonably necessary for the transmission of the information or the accomplishment of the purpose for which the lawyer is consulted, and includes a legal opinion formed and the advice given by the lawyer in the course of that relationship.
CONFRONTATION - Witness testifying in presence of defendant.
CONSANGUINITY - Blood relationship.
CONSIGN - To give in charge; commit; entrust; to send or transmit goods to a merchant, factor, or agent for sale.
CONSIGNEE - One to whom a consignment is made.
CONSIGNOR - One who sends or makes a consignment.
CONSPIRACY - In criminal law, it means an agreement between two or more persons to commit an unlawful act.
CONSPIRATORS - Persons involved in a conspiracy.
CONSTITUTION - The fundamental law of a nation or state.
CONSTRUCTION OF GENDERS - The masculine gender includes the feminine and neuter.
CONSTRUCTION OF SINGULAR AND PLURAL - The singular number includes the plural; and the plural, the singular.
CONSTRUCTION OF TENSES - The present tense includes the past and future tenses; and the future, the present.
CONSTRUCTIVE - An act or condition assumed from other parts or conditions.
CONSTRUE - To ascertain the meaning of language.
CONSUMMATE - To complete.
CONTIGUOUS - Adjoining; touching; bounded by.
CONTINGENT - Possible, but not assured; dependent upon some condition.
CONTINUANCE - The adjournment or postponement of an action pending in a court.
CONTRA - Against, opposed to; contrary.
CONTRACT - An agreement between two or more persons to do or not to do a particular thing.
CONTROVERT - To dispute, deny.
CONVERSION - Dealing with the personal property of another as if it were one's own, without right.
CONVEYANCE - An instrument transferring title to land.
CONVICTION - Generally, the result of a criminal trial which ends in a judgment or sentence that the defendant is guilty as charged.

COOPERATIVE - A cooperative is a voluntary organization of persons with a common interest, formed and operated along democratic lines for the purpose of supplying services at cost to its members and other patrons, who contribute both capital and business.
CORPUS DELICTI - The body of a crime; the crime itself.
CORROBORATE - To strengthen; to add weight by additional evidence.
COUNTERCLAIM - A claim presented by a defendant in opposition to or deduction from the claim of the plaintiff.
COUNTY - Political subdivision of a state.
COVENANT - Agreement.
CREDIBLE - Worthy of belief.
CREDITOR - A person to whom a debt is owing by another person, called the "debtor."
CRIMINAL ACTION - Includes criminal proceedings.
CRIMINAL INFORMATION - Same as complaint.
CRITERION (sing.)
CRITERIA (plural) - A means or tests for judging; a standard or standards.
CROSS-EXAMINATION - Examination of a witness by a party other than the direct examiner upon a matter that is within the scope of the direct examination of the witness.
CULPABLE - Blamable.
CY-PRES - As near as (possible). The rule of *cy-pres* is a rule for the construction of instruments in equity by which the intention of the party is carried out *as near as may be*, when it would be impossible or illegal to give it literal effect.

D

DAMAGES - A monetary compensation, which may be recovered in the courts by any person who has suffered loss, or injury, whether to his person, property or rights through the unlawful act or omission or negligence of another.
DECLARANT - A person who makes a statement.
DE FACTO - In fact; actually but without legal authority.
DE JURE - Of right; legitimate; lawful.
DE MINIMIS - Very small or trifling.
DE NOVO - Anew; afresh; a second time.
DEBT - A specified sum of money owing to one person from another, including not only the obligation of the debtor to pay, but the right of the creditor to receive and enforce payment.
DECEDENT - A dead person.
DECISION - A judgment or decree pronounced by a court in determination of a case.
DECREE - An order of the court, determining the rights of all parties to a suit.
DEED - A writing containing a contract sealed and delivered; particularly to convey real property.
DEFALCATION - Misappropriation of funds.
DEFAMATION - Injuring one's reputation by false statements.
DEFAULT - The failure to fulfill a duty, observe a promise, discharge an obligation, or perform an agreement.
DEFENDANT - The person defending or denying; the party against whom relief or recovery is sought in an action or suit.
DEFRAUD - To practice fraud; to cheat or trick.
DELEGATE (v.)- To entrust to the care or management of another.
DELICTUS - A crime.
DEMUR (v.) - To dispute the sufficiency in law of the pleading of the other side.

DEMURRAGE - In maritime law, it means, the sum fixed or allowed as remuneration to the owners of a ship for the detention of their vessel beyond the number of days allowed for loading and unloading or for sailing; also used in railroad terminology.
DENIAL - A form of pleading; refusing to admit the truth of a statement, charge, etc.
DEPONENT - One who gives testimony under oath reduced to writing.
DEPOSITION - Testimony given under oath outside of court for use in court or for the purpose of obtaining information in preparation for trial of a case.
DETERIORATION - A degeneration such as from decay, corrosion or disintegration.
DETRIMENT - Any loss or harm to person or property.
DEVIATION - A turning aside.
DEVISE - A gift of real property by the last will and testament of the donor.
DICTUM (sing.)
DICTA (plural) - Any statements made by the court in an opinion concerning some rule of law not necessarily involved nor essential to the determination of the case.
DIRECT EVIDENCE - Evidence that directly proves a fact, without an inference or presumption, and which in itself if true, conclusively establishes that fact.
DIRECT EXAMINATION - The first examination of a witness upon a matter that is not within the scope of a previous examination of the witness.
DISAFFIRM - To repudiate.
DISMISS - In an action or suit, it means to dispose of the case without any further consideration or hearing.
DISSENT - To denote disagreement of one or more judges of a court with the decision passed by the majority upon a case before them.
DOCKET (n.) - A formal record, entered in brief, of the proceedings in a court.
DOCTRINE - A rule, principle, theory of law.
DOMICILE - That place where a man has his true, fixed and permanent home to which whenever he is absent he has the intention of returning.
DRAFT (n.) - A commercial paper ordering payment of money drawn by one person on another.
DRAWEE - The person who is requested to pay the money.
DRAWER - The person who draws the commercial paper and addresses it to the drawee.
DUPLICATE - A counterpart produced by the same impression as the original enlargements and miniatures, or by mechanical or electronic re-recording, or by chemical reproduction, or by other equivalent technique which accurately reproduces the original.
DURESS - Use of force to compel performance or non-performance of an act.

E

EASEMENT - A liberty, privilege, or advantage without profit, in the lands of another.
EGRESS - Act or right of going out or leaving; emergence.
EIUSDEM GENERIS - Of the same kind, class or nature. A rule used in the construction of language in a legal document.
EMBEZZLEMENT - To steal; to appropriate fraudulently to one's own use property entrusted to one's care.
EMBRACERY - Unlawful attempt to influence jurors, etc., but not by offering value.
EMINENT DOMAIN - The right of a state to take private property for public use.
ENACT - To make into a law.
ENDORSEMENT - Act of writing one's name on the back of a note, bill or similar written instrument.

ENJOIN - To require a person, by writ of injunction from a court of equity, to perform or to abstain or desist from some act.
ENTIRETY - The whole; that which the law considers as one whole, and not capable of being divided into parts.
ENTRAPMENT - Inducing one to commit a crime so as to arrest him.
ENUMERATED - Mentioned specifically; designated.
ENURE - To operate or take effect.
EQUITY - In its broadest sense, this term denotes the spirit and the habit of fairness, justness, and right dealing which regulate the conduct of men.
ERROR - A mistake of law, or the false or irregular application of law as will nullify the judicial proceedings.
ESCROW - A deed, bond or other written engagement, delivered to a third person, to be delivered by him only upon the performance or fulfillment of some condition.
ESTATE - The interest which any one has in lands, or in any other subject of property.
ESTOP - To stop, bar, or impede.
ESTOPPEL - A rule of law which prevents a man from alleging or denying a fact, because of his own previous act.
ET AL. (alii) - And others.
ET SEQ. (sequential) - And the following.
ET UX. (uxor) - And wife.
EVIDENCE - Testimony, writings, material objects, or other things presented to the senses that are offered to prove the existence or non-existence of a fact.
Means from which inferences may be drawn as a basis of proof in duly constituted judicial or fact finding tribunals, and includes testimony in the form of opinion and hearsay.
EX CONTRACTU
EX DELICTO - In law, rights and causes of action are divided into two classes, those arising *ex contractu* (from a contract) and those arising *ex delicto* (from a delict or tort).
EX OFFICIO - From office; by virtue of the office.
EX PARTE - On one side only; by or for one.
EX POST FACTO - After the fact.
EX POST FACTO LAW - A law passed after an act was done which retroactively makes such act a crime.
EX REL. (relations) - Upon relation or information.
EXCEPTION - An objection upon a matter of law to a decision made, either before or after judgment by a court.
EXECUTOR (male)
EXECUTRIX (female) - A person who has been appointed by will to execute the will.
EXECUTORY - That which is yet to be executed or performed.
EXEMPT - To release from some liability to which others are subject.
EXONERATION - The removal of a burden, charge or duty.
EXTRADITION - Surrender of a fugitive from one nation to another.

F

F.A.S.- "Free alongside ship"; delivery at dock for ship named.
F.O.B.- "Free on board"; seller will deliver to car, truck, vessel, or other conveyance by which goods are to be transported, without expense or risk of loss to the buyer or consignee.
FABRICATE - To construct; to invent a false story.
FACSIMILE - An exact or accurate copy of an original instrument.

FACTOR - A commercial agent.
FEASANCE - The doing of an act.
FELONIOUS - Criminal, malicious.
FELONY - Generally, a criminal offense that may be punished by death or imprisonment for more than one year as differentiated from a misdemeanor.
FEME SOLE - A single woman.
FIDUCIARY - A person who is invested with rights and powers to be exercised for the benefit of another person.
FIERI FACIAS - A writ of execution commanding the sheriff to levy and collect the amount of a judgment from the goods and chattels of the judgment debtor.
FINDING OF FACT - Determination from proof or judicial notice of the existence of a fact. A ruling implies a supporting finding of fact; no separate or formal finding is required unless required by a statute of this state.
FISCAL - Relating to accounts or the management of revenue.
FORECLOSURE (sale) - A sale of mortgaged property to obtain satisfaction of the mortgage out of the sale proceeds.
FORFEITURE - A penalty, a fine.
FORGERY - Fabricating or producing falsely, counterfeited.
FORTUITOUS - Accidental.
FORUM - A court of justice; a place of jurisdiction.
FRAUD - Deception; trickery.
FREEHOLDER - One who owns real property.
FUNGIBLE - Of such kind or nature that one specimen or part may be used in the place of another.

G

GARNISHEE - Person garnished.
GARNISHMENT - A legal process to reach the money or effects of a defendant, in the possession or control of a third person.
GRAND JURY - Not less than 16, not more than 23 citizens of a county sworn to inquire into crimes committed or triable in the county.
GRANT - To agree to; convey, especially real property.
GRANTEE - The person to whom a grant is made.
GRANTOR - The person by whom a grant is made.
GRATUITOUS - Given without a return, compensation or consideration.
GRAVAMEN - The grievance complained of or the substantial cause of a criminal action.
GUARANTY (n.) - A promise to answer for the payment of some debt, or the performance of some duty, in case of the failure of another person, who, in the first instance, is liable for such payment or performance.
GUARDIAN - The person, committee, or other representative authorized by law to protect the person or estate or both of an incompetent (or of a *sui juris* person having a guardian) and to act for him in matters affecting his person or property or both. An incompetent is a person under disability imposed by law.
GUILTY - Establishment of the fact that one has committed a breach of conduct; especially, a violation of law.

H

HABEAS CORPUS - You have the body; the name given to a variety of writs, having for their object to bring a party before a court or judge for decision as to whether such person is being lawfully held prisoner.
HABENDUM - In conveyancing; it is the clause in a deed conveying land which defines the extent of ownership to be held by the grantee.
HEARING - A proceeding whereby the arguments of the interested parties are heared.
HEARSAY - A type of testimony given by a witness who relates, not what he knows personally, but what others have told hi, or what he has heard said by others.
HEARSAY RULE, THE - (a) "Hearsay evidence" is evidence of a statement that was made other than by a witness while testifying at the hearing and that is offered to prove the truth of the matter stated; (b) Except as provided by law, hearsay evidence is inadmissible; (c) This section shall be known and may be cited as the hearsay rule.
HEIR - Generally, one who inherits property, real or personal.
HOLDER OF THE PRIVILEGE - (a) The client when he has no guardian or conservator; (b) A guardian or conservator of the client when the client has a guardian or conservator; (c) The personal representative of the client if the client is dead; (d) A successor, assign, trustee in dissolution, or any similar representative of a firm, association, organization, partnership, business trust, corporation, or public entity that is no longer in existence.
HUNG JURY - One so divided that they can't agree on a verdict.
HUSBAND-WIFE PRIVILEGE - An accused in a criminal proceeding has a privilege to prevent his spouse from testifying against him.
HYPOTHECATE - To pledge a thing without delivering it to the pledgee.
HYPOTHESIS - A supposition, assumption, or toehry.

I

I.E. (id est) - That is.
IB., OR IBID.(ibidem) - In the same place; used to refer to a legal reference previously cited to avoid repeating the entire citation.
ILLICIT - Prohibited; unlawful.
ILLUSORY - Deceiving by false appearance.
IMMUNITY - Exemption.
IMPEACH - To accuse, to dispute.
IMPEDIMENTS - Disabilities, or hindrances.
IMPLEAD - To sue or prosecute by due course of law.
IMPUTED - Attributed or charged to.
IN LOCO PARENTIS - In place of parent, a guardian.
IN TOTO - In the whole; completely.
INCHOATE - Imperfect; unfinished.
INCOMMUNICADO - Denial of the right of a prisoner to communicate with friends or relatives.
INCOMPETENT - One who is incapable of caring for his own affairs because he is mentally deficient or undeveloped.
INCRIMINATION - A matter will incriminate a person if it constitutes, or forms an essential part of, or, taken in connection with other matters disclosed, is a basis for a reasonable inference of such a violation of the laws of this State as to subject him to liability to punishment therefor, unless he has become for any reason permanently immune from punishment for such violation.
INCUMBRANCE - Generally a claim, lien, charge or liability attached to and binding real property.

INDEMNIFY - To secure against loss or damage; also, to make reimbursement to one for a loss already incurred by him.
INDEMNITY - An agreement to reimburse another person in case of an anticipated loss falling upon him.
INDICIA - Signs; indications.
INDICTMENT - An accusation in writing found and presented by a grand jury charging that a person has committed a crime.
INDORSE - To write a name on the back of a legal paper or document, generally, a negotiable instrument
INDUCEMENT - Cause or reason why a thing is done or that which incites the person to do the act or commit a crime; the motive for the criminal act.
INFANT - In civil cases one under 21 years of age.
INFORMATION - A formal accusation of crime made by a prosecuting attorney.
INFRA - Below, under; this word occurring by itself in a publication refers the reader to a future part of the publication.
INGRESS - The act of going into.
INJUNCTION - A writ or order by the court requiring a person, generally, to do or to refrain from doing an act.
INSOLVENT - The condition of a person who is unable to pay his debts.
INSTRUCTION - A direction given by the judge to the jury concerning the law of the case.
INTERIM - In the meantime; time intervening.
INTERLOCUTORY - Temporary, not final; something intervening between the commencement and the end of a suit which decides some point or matter, but is not a final decision of the whole controversy.
INTERROGATORIES - A series of formal written questions used in the examination of a party or a witness usually prior to a trial.
INTESTATE - A person who dies without a will.
INURE - To result, to take effect.
IPSO FACTO - By the fact iself; by the mere fact.
ISSUE (n.) The disputed point or question in a case,

J

JEOPARDY - Danger, hazard, peril.
JOINDER - Joining; uniting with another person in some legal steps or proceeding.
JOINT - United; combined.
JUDGE - Member or members or representative or representatives of a court conducting a trial or hearing at which evidence is introduced.
JUDGMENT - The official decision of a court of justice.
JUDICIAL OR JUDICIARY - Relating to or connected with the administration of justice.
JURAT - The clause written at the foot of an affidavit, stating when, where and before whom such affidavit was sworn.
JURISDICTION - The authority to hear and determine controversies between parties.
JURISPRUDENCE - The philosophy of law.
JURY - A body of persons legally selected to inquire into any matter of fact, and to render their verdict according to the evidence.

L

LACHES - The failure to diligently assert a right, which results in a refusal to allow relief.

LANDLORD AND TENANT - A phrase used to denote the legal relation existing between the owner and occupant of real estate.

LARCENY - Stealing personal property belonging to another.

LATENT - Hidden; that which does not appear on the face of a thing.

LAW - Includes constitutional, statutory, and decisional law.

LAWYER-CLIENT PRIVILEGE - (1) A "client" is a person, public officer, or corporation, association, or other organization or entity, either public or private, who is rendered professional legal services by a lawyer, or who consults a lawyer with a view to obtaining professional legal services from him; (2) A "lawyer" is a person authorized, or reasonably believed by the client to be authorized, to practice law in any state or nation; (3) A "representative of the lawyer" is one employed to assist the lawyer in the rendition of professional legal services; (4) A communication is "confidential" if not intended to be disclosed to third persons other than those to whom disclosure is in furtherance of the rendition of professional legal services to the client or those reasonably necessary for the transmission of the communication.

General rule of privilege - A client has a privilege to refuse to disclose and to prevent any other person from disclosing confidential communications made for the purpose of facilitating the rendition of professional legal services to the client, (1) between himself or his representative and his lawyer or his lawyer's representative, or (2) between his lawyer and the lawyer's representative, or (3) by him or his lawyer to a lawyer representing another in a matter of common interest, or (4) between representatives of the client or between the client and a representative of the client, or (5) between lawyers representing the client.

LEADING QUESTION - Question that suggests to the witness the answer that the examining party desires.

LEASE - A contract by which one conveys real estate for a limited time usually for a specified rent; personal property also may be leased.

LEGISLATION - The act of enacting laws.

LEGITIMATE - Lawful.

LESSEE - One to whom a lease is given.

LESSOR - One who grants a lease

LEVY - A collecting or exacting by authority.

LIABLE - Responsible; bound or obligated in law or equity.

LIBEL (v.) - To defame or injure a person's reputation by a published writing.

(n.) - The initial pleading on the part of the plaintiff in an admiralty proceeding.

LIEN - A hold or claim which one person has upon the property of another as a security for some debt or charge.

LIQUIDATED - Fixed; settled.

LIS PENDENS - A pending civil or criminal action.

LITERAL - According to the language.

LITIGANT - A party to a lawsuit.

LITATION - A judicial controversy.

LOCUS - A place.

LOCUS DELICTI - Place of the crime.

LOCUS POENITENTIAE - The abandoning or giving up of one's intention to commit some crime before it is fully completed or abandoning a conspiracy before its purpose is accomplished.

M

MALFEASANCE - To do a wrongful act.

MALICE - The doing of a wrongful act Intentionally without just cause or excuse.

MANDAMUS - The name of a writ issued by a court to enforce the performance of some public duty.
MANDATORY (adj.) Containing a command.
MARITIME - Pertaining to the sea or to commerce thereon.
MARSHALING - Arranging or disposing of in order.
MAXIM - An established principle or proposition.
MINISTERIAL - That which involves obedience to instruction, but demands no special discretion, judgment or skill.
MISAPPROPRIATE - Dealing fraudulently with property entrusted to one.
MISDEMEANOR - A crime less than a felony and punishable by a fine or imprisonment for less than one year.
MISFEASANCE - Improper performance of a lawful act.
MISREPRESENTATION - An untrue representation of facts.
MITIGATE - To make or become less severe, harsh.
MITTIMUS - A warrant of commitment to prison.
MOOT (adj.) Unsettled, undecided, not necessary to be decided.
MORTGAGE - A conveyance of property upon condition, as security for the payment of a debt or the performance of a duty, and to become void upon payment or performance according to the stipulated terms.
MORTGAGEE - A person to whom property is mortgaged.
MORTGAGOR - One who gives a mortgage.
MOTION - In legal proceedings, a "motion" is an application, either written or oral, addressed to the court by a party to an action or a suit requesting the ruling of the court on a matter of law.
MUTUALITY - Reciprocation.

N

NEGLIGENCE - The failure to exercise that degree of care which an ordinarily prudent person would exercise under like circumstances.
NEGOTIABLE (instrument) - Any instrument obligating the payment of money which is transferable from one person to another by endorsement and delivery or by delivery only.
NEGOTIATE - To transact business; to transfer a negotiable instrument; to seek agreement for the amicable disposition of a controversy or case.
NOLLE PROSEQUI - A formal entry upon the record, by the plaintiff in a civil suit or the prosecuting officer in a criminal action, by which he declares that he "will no further prosecute" the case.
NOLO CONTENDERE - The name of a plea in a criminal action, having the same effect as a plea of guilty; but not constituting a direct admission of guilt.
NOMINAL - Not real or substantial.
NOMINAL DAMAGES - Award of a trifling sum where no substantial injury is proved to have been sustained.
NONFEASANCE - Neglect of duty.
NOVATION - The substitution of a new debt or obligation for an existing one.
NUNC PRO TUNC - A phrase applied to acts allowed to be done after the time when they should be done, with a retroactive effect.("Now for then.")

O

OATH - Oath includes affirmation or declaration under penalty of perjury.
OBITER DICTUM - Opinion expressed by a court on a matter not essentially involved in a case and hence not a decision; also called dicta, if plural.

OBJECT (v.) - To oppose as improper or illegal and referring the question of its propriety or legality to the court.

OBLIGATION - A legal duty, by which a person is bound to do or not to do a certain thing.

OBLIGEE - The person to whom an obligation is owed.

OBLIGOR - The person who is to perform the obligation.

OFFER (v.) - To present for acceptance or rejection.

(n.) - A proposal to do a thing, usually a proposal to make a contract.

OFFICIAL INFORMATION - Information within the custody or control of a department or agency of the government the disclosure of which is shown to be contrary to the public interest.

OFFSET - A deduction.

ONUS PROBANDI - Burden of proof.

OPINION - The statement by a judge of the decision reached in a case, giving the law as applied to the case and giving reasons for the judgment; also a belief or view.

OPTION - The exercise of the power of choice; also a privilege existing in one person, for which he has paid money, which gives him the right to buy or sell real or personal property at a given price within a specified time.

ORDER - A rule or regulation; every direction of a court or judge made or entered in writing but not including a judgment.

ORDINANCE - Generally, a rule established by authority; also commonly used to designate the legislative acts of a municipal corporation.

ORIGINAL - Writing or recording itself or any counterpart intended to have the same effect by a person executing or issuing it. An "original" of a photograph includes the negative or any print therefrom. If data are stored in a computer or similar device, any printout or other output readable by sight, shown to reflect the data accurately, is an "original."

OVERT - Open, manifest.

P

PANEL - A group of jurors selected to serve during a term of the court.

PARENS PATRIAE - Sovereign power of a state to protect or be a guardian over children and incompetents.

PAROL - Oral or verbal.

PAROLE - To release one in prison before the expiration of his sentence, conditionally.

PARITY - Equality in purchasing power between the farmer and other segments of the economy.

PARTITION - A legal division of real or personal property between one or more owners.

PARTNERSHIP - An association of two or more persons to carry on as co-owners a business for profit.

PATENT (adj.) - Evident.

(n.) - A grant of some privilege, property, or authority, made by the government or sovereign of a country to one or more individuals.

PECULATION - Stealing.

PECUNIARY - Monetary.

PENULTIMATE - Next to the last.

PER CURIAM - A phrase used in the report of a decision to distinguish an opinion of the whole court from an opinion written by any one judge.

PER SE - In itself; taken alone.

PERCEIVE - To acquire knowledge through one's senses.

PEREMPTORY - Imperative; absolute.

PERJURY - To lie or state falsely under oath.

PERPETUITY - Perpetual existence; also the quality or condition of an estate limited so that it will not take effect or vest within the period fixed by law.
PERSON - Includes a natural person, firm, association, organization, partnership, business trust, corporation, or public entity.
PERSONAL PROPERTY - Includes money, goods, chattels, things in action, and evidences of debt.
PERSONALTY - Short term for personal property.
PETITION - An application in writing for an order of the court, stating the circumstances upon which it is founded and requesting any order or other relief from a court.
PLAINTIFF - A person who brings a court action.
PLEA - A pleading in a suit or action.
PLEADINGS - Formal allegations made by the parties of their respective claims and defenses, for the judgment of the court.
PLEDGE - A deposit of personal property as a security for the performance of an act.
PLEDGEE - The party to whom goods are delivered in pledge.
PLEDGOR - The party delivering goods in pledge.
PLENARY - Full; complete.
POLICE POWER - Inherent power of the state or its political subdivisions to enact laws within constitutional limits to promote the general welfare of society or the community.
POLLING THE JURY - Call the names of persons on a jury and requiring each juror to declare what his verdict is before it is legally recorded.
POST MORTEM - After death.
POWER OF ATTORNEY - A writing authorizing one to act for another.
PRECEPT - An order, warrant, or writ issued to an officer or body of officers, commanding him or them to do some act within the scope of his or their powers.
PRELIMINARY FACT - Fact upon the existence or nonexistence of which depends the admissibility or inadmissibility of evidence. The phrase "the admissibility or inadmissibility of evidence" includes the qualification or disqualification of a person to be a witness and the existence or nonexistence of a privilege.
PREPONDERANCE - Outweighing.
PRESENTMENT - A report by a grand jury on something they have investigated on their own knowledge.
PRESUMPTION - An assumption of fact resulting from a rule of law which requires such fact to be assumed from another fact or group of facts found or otherwise established in the action.
PRIMA FACUE - At first sight.
PRIMA FACIE CASE - A case where the evidence is very patent against the defendant.
PRINCIPAL - The source of authority or rights; a person primarily liable as differentiated from "principle" as a primary or basic doctrine.
PRO AND CON - For and against.
PRO RATA - Proportionally.
PROBATE - Relating to proof, especially to the proof of wills.
PROBATIVE - Tending to prove.
PROCEDURE - In law, this term generally denotes rules which are established by the Federal, State, or local Governments regarding the types of pleading and courtroom practice which must be followed by the parties involved in a criminal or civil case.
PROCLAMATION - A public notice by an official of some order, intended action, or state of facts.

PROFFERED EVIDENCE - The admissibility or inadmissibility of which is dependent upon the existence or nonexistence of a preliminary fact.
PROMISSORY (NOTE) - A promise in writing to pay a specified sum at an expressed time, or on demand, or at sight, to a named person, or to his order, or bearer.
PROOF - The establishment by evidence of a requisite degree of belief concerning a fact in the mind of the trier of fact or the court.
PROPERTY - Includes both real and personal property.
PROPRIETARY (adj.) - Relating or pertaining to ownership; usually a single owner.
PROSECUTE - To carry on an action or other judicial proceeding; to proceed against a person criminally.
PROVISO - A limitation or condition in a legal instrument.
PROXIMATE - Immediate; nearest
PUBLIC EMPLOYEE - An officer, agent, or employee of a public entity.
PUBLIC ENTITY - Includes a national, state, county, city and county, city, district, public authority, public agency, or any other political subdivision or public corporation, whether foreign or domestic.
PUBLIC OFFICIAL - Includes an official of a political dubdivision of such state or territory and of a municipality.
PUNITIVE - Relating to punishment.

Q

QUASH - To make void.
QUASI - As if; as it were.
QUID PRO QUO - Something for something; the giving of one valuable thing for another.
QUITCLAIM (v.) - To release or relinquish claim or title to, especially in deeds to realty.
QUO WARRANTO - A legal procedure to test an official's right to a public office or the right to hold a franchise, or to hold an office in a domestic corporation.

R

RATIFY - To approve and sanction.
REAL PROPERTY - Includes lands, tenements, and hereditaments.
REALTY - A brief term for real property.
REBUT - To contradict; to refute, especially by evidence and arguments.
RECEIVER - A person who is appointed by the court to receive, and hold in trust property in litigation.
RECIDIVIST - Habitual criminal.
RECIPROCAL - Mutual.
RECOUPMENT - To keep back or get something which is due; also, it is the right of a defendant to have a deduction from the amount of the plaintiff's damages because the plaintiff has not fulfilled his part of the same contract.
RECROSS EXAMINATION - Examination of a witness by a cross-examiner subsequent to a redirect examination of the witness.
REDEEM - To release an estate or article from mortgage or pledge by paying the debt for which it stood as security.
REDIRECT EXAMINATION - Examination of a witness by the direct examiner subsequent to the cross-examination of the witness.
REFEREE - A person to whom a cause pending in a court is referred by the court, to take testimony, hear the parties, and report thereon to the court.

REFERENDUM - A method of submitting an important legislative or administrative matter to a direct vote of the people.
RELEVANT EVIDENCE - Evidence including evidence relevant to the credulity of a witness or hearsay declarant, having any tendency in reason to prove or disprove any disputed fact that is of consequence to the determination of the action.
REMAND - To send a case back to the lower court from which it came, for further proceedings.
REPLEVIN - An action to recover goods or chattels wrongfully taken or detained.
REPLY (REPLICATION) - Generally, a reply is what the plaintiff or other person who has instituted proceedings says in answer to the defendant's case.
RE JUDICATA - A thing judicially acted upon or decided.
RES ADJUDICATA - Doctrine that an issue or dispute litigated and determined in a case between the opposing parties is deemed permanently decided between these parties.
RESCIND (RECISSION) - To avoid or cancel a contract.
RESPONDENT - A defendant in a proceeding in chancery or admiralty; also, the person who contends against the appeal in a case.
RESTITUTION - In equity, it is the restoration of both parties to their original condition (when practicable), upon the rescission of a contract for fraud or similar cause.
RETROACTIVE (RETROSPECTIVE) - Looking back; effective as of a prior time.
REVERSED - A term used by appellate courts to indicate that the decision of the lower court in the case before it has been set aside.
REVOKE - To recall or cancel.
RIPARIAN (RIGHTS) - The rights of a person owning land containing or bordering on a water course or other body of water, such as lakes and rivers.

S

SALE - A contract whereby the ownership of property is transferred from one person to another for a sum of money or for any consideration.
SANCTION - A penalty or punishment provided as a means of enforcing obedience to a law; also, an authorization.
SATISFACTION - The discharge of an obligation by paying a party what is due to him; or what is awarded to him by the judgment of a court or otherwise.
SCIENTER - Knowingly; also, it is used in pleading to denote the defendant's guilty knowledge.
SCINTILLA - A spark; also the least particle.
SECRET OF STATE - Governmental secret relating to the national defense or the international relations of the United States.
SECURITY - Indemnification; the term is applied to an obligation, such as a mortgage or deed of trust, given by a debtor to insure the payment or performance of his debt, by furnishing the creditor with a resource to be used in case of the debtor's failure to fulfill the principal obligation.
SENTENCE - The judgment formally pronounced by the court or judge upon the defendant after his conviction in a criminal prosecution.
SET-OFF - A claim or demand which one party in an action credits against the claim of the opposing party.
SHALL and MAY - "Shall" is mandatory and "may" is permissive.
SITUS - Location.
SOVEREIGN - A person, body or state in which independent and supreme authority is vested.
STARE DECISIS - To follow decided cases.

STATE - "State" means this State, unless applied to the different parts of the United States. In the latter case, it includes any state, district, commonwealth, territory or insular possession of the United States, including the District of Columbia.
STATEMENT - (a) Oral or written verbal expression or (b) nonverbal conduct of a person intended by him as a substitute for oral or written verbal expression.
STATUTE - An act of the legislature. Includes a treaty.
STATUTE OF LIMITATION - A statute limiting the time to bring an action after the right of action has arisen.
STAY - To hold in abeyance an order of a court.
STIPULATION - Any agreement made by opposing attorneys regulating any matter incidental to the proceedings or trial.
SUBORDINATION (AGREEMENT) - An agreement making one's rights inferior to or of a lower rank than another's.
SUBORNATION - The crime of procuring a person to lie or to make false statements to a court.
SUBPOENA - A writ or order directed to a person, and requiring his attendance at a particular time and place to testify as a witness.
SUBPOENA DUCES TECUM - A subpoena used, not only for the purpose of compelling witnesses to attend in court, but also requiring them to bring with them books or documents which may be in their possession, and which may tend to elucidate the subject matter of the trial.
SUBROGATION - The substituting of one for another as a creditor, the new creditor succeeding to the former's rights.
SUBSIDY - A government grant to assist a private enterprise deemed advantageous to the public.
SUI GENERIS - Of the same kind.
SUIT - Any civil proceeding by a person or persons against another or others in a court of justice by which the plaintiff pursues the remedies afforded him by law.
SUMMONS - A notice to a defendant that an action against him has been commenced and requiring him to appear in court and answer the complaint.
SUPRA - Above; this word occurring by itself in a book refers the reader to a previous part of the book.
SURETY - A person who binds himself for the payment of a sum of money, or for the performance of something else, for another.
SURPLUSAGE - Extraneous or unnecessary matter.
SURVIVORSHIP - A term used when a person becomes entitled to property by reason of his having survived another person who had an interest in the property.
SUSPEND SENTENCE - Hold back a sentence pending good behavior of prisoner.
SYLLABUS - A note prefixed to a report, especially a case, giving a brief statement of the court's ruling on different issues of the case.

T

TALESMAN - Person summoned to fill a panel of jurors.
TENANT - One who holds or possesses lands by any kind of right or title; also, one who has the temporary use and occupation of real property owned by another person (landlord), the duration and terms of his tenancy being usually fixed by an instrument called "a lease."
TENDER - An offer of money; an expression of willingness to perform a contract according to its terms.
TERM - When used with reference to a court, it signifies the period of time during which the court holds a session, usually of several weeks or months duration.

TESTAMENTARY - Pertaining to a will or the administration of a will.
TESTATOR (male)
TESTATRIX (female) - One who makes or has made a testament or will.
TESTIFY (TESTIMONY) - To give evidence under oath as a witness.
TO WIT - That is to say; namely.
TORT - Wrong; injury to the person.
TRANSITORY - Passing from place to place.
TRESPASS - Entry into another's ground, illegally.
TRIAL - The examination of a cause, civil or criminal, before a judge who has jurisdiction over it, according to the laws of the land.
TRIER OF FACT - Includes (a) the jury and (b) the court when the court is trying an issue of fact other than one relating to the admissibility of evidence.
TRUST - A right of property, real or personal, held by one party for the benefit of another.
TRUSTEE - One who lawfully holds property in custody for the benefit of another.

U

UNAVAILABLE AS A WITNESS - The declarant is (1) Exempted or precluded on the ground of privilege from testifying concerning the matter to which his statement is relevant; (2) Disqualified from testifying to the matter; (3) Dead or unable to attend or to testify at the hearing because of then existing physical or mental illness or infirmity; (4) Absent from the hearing and the court is unable to compel his attendance by its process; or (5) Absent from the hearing and the proponent of his statement has exercised reasonable diligence but has been unable to procure his attendance by the court's process.
ULTRA VIRES - Acts beyond the scope and power of a corporation, association, etc.
UNILATERAL - One-sided; obligation upon, or act of one party.
USURY - Unlawful interest on a loan.

V

VACATE - To set aside; to move out.
VARIANCE - A discrepancy or disagreement between two instruments or two aspects of the same case, which by law should be consistent.
VENDEE - A purchaser or buyer.
VENDOR - The person who transfers property by sale, particularly real estate; the term "seller" is used more commonly for one who sells personal property.
VENIREMEN - Persons ordered to appear to serve on a jury or composing a panel of jurors.
VENUE - The place at which an action is tried, generally based on locality or judicial district in which an injury occurred or a material fact happened.
VERDICT - The formal decision or finding of a jury.
VERIFY - To confirm or substantiate by oath.
VEST - To accrue to.
VOID - Having no legal force or binding effect.
VOIR DIRE - Preliminary examination of a witness or a juror to test competence, interest, prejudice, etc.

W

WAIVE - To give up a right.
WAIVER - The intentional or voluntary relinquishment of a known right.
WARRANT (WARRANTY) (v.) - To promise that a certain fact or state of facts, in relation to the subject matter, is, or shall be, as it is represented to be.

WARRANT (n.) - A writ issued by a judge, or other competent authority, addressed to a sheriff, or other officer, requiring him to arrest the person therein named, and bring him before the judge or court to answer or be examined regarding the offense with which he is charged.

WRIT - An order or process issued in the name of the sovereign or in the name of a court or judicial officer, commanding the performance or nonperformance of some act.

WRITING - Handwriting, typewriting, printing, photostating, photographing and every other means of recording upon any tangible thing any form of communication or representation, including letters, words, pictures, sounds, or symbols, or combinations thereof.

WRITINGS AND RECORDINGS - Consists of letters, words, or numbers, or their equivalent, set down by handwriting, typewriting, printing, photostating, photographing, magnetic impulse, mechanical or electronic recording, or other form of data compilation.

Y

YEA AND NAY - Yes and no.

YELLOW DOG CONTRACT - A contract by which employer requires employee to sign an instrument promising as condition that he will not join a union during its continuance, and will be discharged if he does join.

Z

ZONING - The division of a city by legislative regulation into districts and the prescription and application in each district of regulations having to do with structural and architectural designs of buildings and of regulations prescribing use to which buildings within designated districts may be put.

www.ingramcontent.com/pod-product-compliance
Lightning Source LLC
Chambersburg PA
CBHW082234120226
39641CB00045B/1309